PALM SPRINGS-STYLE GARDENING

The Complete Guide to Plants and Practices

for Gorgeous Dryland Gardens

PALM SPRINGS-STYLE GARDENING

The Complete Guide to Plants and Practices
for Gorgeous Dryland Gardens

by Maureen Gilmer

SUNBELT PUBLICATIONS | SAN DIEGO, CALIFORNIA

PALM SPRINGS-STYLE GARDENING

Sunbelt Publications, Inc

Copyright © 2009 by Maureen Gilmer

All rights reserved. First edition 2009

Edited by Jennifer Redmond
Cover and book design by Kathleen Wise
Various graphic elements © istockphoto.com/browndog studios, Illusime, LoBoCo, Pingwin, N-L, Sunygraphics, Talshiar
Printed in China

Sunbelt Publications, Inc.
P.O. Box 191126
San Diego, CA 92159-1126
(619) 258-4911, fax: (619) 258-4916
www.sunbeltbooks.com

13 12 11 10 09   5 4 3 2 1

Library of Congress Cataloging-in-Publication Data

Gilmer, Maureen.
Palm Springs-style gardening : the complete guide to plants and practices
for gorgeous dryland gardens / by Maureen Gilmer.—1st ed.
    p. cm.
Includes index.
ISBN 978-0-932653-89-5
1. Desert gardening—California. 2. Desert plants—California. I. Title.
II. Title: Complete guide to plants and practices for gorgeous dryland gardens.
 SB427.5.G55 2009
 635.9'52509795--dc22
                            2008036881

All photographs by the author unless noted. Cover photo: Kathleen Wise

DEDICATION

This book is dedicated to everyone who understands just how precious our dwindling resources are here in the arid west, and those who will come to this same realization and choose to garden accordingly. It is my hope that these pages will offer them the tools needed to set a new standard for our regional aesthetic that works with nature rather than taking from her. Perhaps if we all took a fresh look at the way we live in this dry climate, we might discover a new path toward a healthy sustainable lifestyle that ensures a greener, more renewable world for ourselves and future generations.

ACKNOWLEDGMENTS

I would like to express my deepest appreciation to those who have helped with this book. If Clark Moorten had not let me dig in his garden and work with his vast collection at Moorten Botanical Garden for four years, I would not have discovered the magic of succulent plants. Thank you to my agent Jeanne Fredericks, Sunbelt editor Jennifer Redmond and the Sunbelt staff. The great contemporary look is the work of Renaissance woman Kathleen Wise, a multi-talented photographer and book designer. My thanks also go out to Dr. Pat and Sue Picchione for their contribution of historic Movie Colony photos, Susan Wallace for allowing me to feature her fabulous bungalow garden, and last but certainly not least, Greg and Katherine Hough for the privilege of shooting and featuring their exquisite Araby home.

TABLE OF CONTENTS

INTRODUCTION

The image of a Palm Springs garden is all about lush backgrounds, intense tropical color, and soft desert palettes. Our mild climate can support a vast array of native and exotic species. But with a rapidly increasing population, hundreds of golf courses and lawns are challenging a finite resource essential to desert life: water. The time has come to follow a more arid landscape style inspired by the character of the desert Southwest.

Dryland gardening has largely been a trial and error effort with a long learning curve. Past preferences for plants and gardens were imported from northern states and areas very different from the desert. This has encouraged a labor- and resource-intensive landscape design. But choosing plants naturally adapted to their climate frees homeowners from a demanding maintenance regime, and perhaps more importantly, it reduces the demand on dwindling resources.

For the last century, the Coachella Valley was inhabited by a few desert-hardy souls and a huge population of seasonal residents. They come in the fall to enjoy our mild winters, then vanish at the start of summer. In recent years an ever-greater population of year-round residents have settled here. They face the same opportunities for gardening as homeowners everywhere, and their efforts have inspired a new approach to the landscape.

Palm Springs-Style Gardening is a guide for homeowners, professionals, and government agencies to better understand this variable aesthetic and learn what plants do well in dryland gardens. It details how to use them to enhance the appeal of specific architectural styles, both traditional and ultra modern. It provides tips and instructions on how to solve problems and cope with climatic extremes to help keep the plants looking their best. Above all, it highlights some of the most water-conservative species that offer all the beauty and color of their thirsty predecessors.

With an extraordinary climate for outdoor living, *al fresco* Palm Springs spaces are created with as much finesse as our interiors. We've grown out of our old palm tree and swimming pool era to expect a more attractive, contemporary and "green" setting for homes large and small. Whether you're a stark modern aficionado or a romantic cottage garden lover, *Palm Springs-Style Gardening* brings the best design ideas, plants, gardening tips, and lifestyle looks together in gorgeous full color beauty.

CHAPTER 1

UNDERSTANDING PLANTS IN THE DESERT

Let's face it, growing plants in a hostile climate with seasons that resemble no others is just counter intuitive. With most valley residents hailing from other parts of the world, very little of what you know about gardening will apply here. In many ways we must rethink the art of the garden, relearn the practice, and discover a whole new palette of plants that grow nowhere else.

Our calendar is crazy. Annual flowers are planted in October and tomatoes at Christmas. During the summer, gardens everywhere are peaking while ours lie semi-dormant, waiting out the heat.

The desert is among the most trying environmental climates in the world. Excessive UV exposure scalds plant leaves. Wind can be persistent and brutal, literally drawing moisture out of foliage at a startling rate. High temperatures can be so stressful that photosynthesis ceases. Even the most durable cacti are challenged.

A TROPICAL DESERT

Technically speaking, our valley floor is classified as a tropical desert. But this is not tropical as in San Diego where the temperatures barely fluctuate day and night from winter to summer. In the desert, the daytime temperature can fall as much as fifty degrees in just a few hours after sunset. Fortunately the lows of midwinter mornings cause only a brief frost that may nip at the bougainvillea, but most plants remain unscathed.

On rare years the cold may be more extensive, as was the case in 2006–07. These years helped to identify plants that are most sensitive to frost damage.

During the social season, which spans October to May, temperatures are moderate, nights cold. In the off season, summer temperatures can reach 120°F, but average about 105 to 110 for the hottest months. Prior to air conditioning most residents left the valley for the summer, and those that remained relied on evaporative cooling. But coolers fail when humidity rises as

OPPOSITE: In select sheltered neighborhoods, tropical plants thrive out of the wind and protected from frost.

To protect from wind and searing heat, old Palm Springs estates feature walled courtyards where conditions can be ten degrees cooler in the depths of summer.

monsoons drift up from Mexico and the desert Southwest. This brings tropical humidity into the valley to create a sticky combination of temperatures in the low 100s and high humidity. These are the most trying conditions for both human beings and plants.

Here in the desert, evergreen plants grow nearly year-round with only a short dormant season, if any. As a result the rate of growth can be astounding for such an arid region if adequate water is provided.

More traditional plants including bedding annuals such as snapdragons and perennials produce their best color in the late winter here. They are tricked into blooming by the high UV light index and warm daytime temperatures. The heat-loving desert plants such as cacti, Mexican birds of paradise, and palms do the majority of their growing in the spring and summer.

The desert is truly an oasis when there is water for plants. This creates a great deal of confusion because nearly everything will grow here, it's just a question of location relative to sun and frost. The way each group adapts to the year-round sunshine is both unique and fascinating. It also demands even the best of us to readjust how we view our gardens.

MEETING THE CHALLENGES OF LOW DESERT GARDENING

☀ SUN

The Coachella Valley enjoys over three hundred days of sunshine per year. The dry air is so lacking in moisture there is little atmosphere to diffuse ultraviolet light, allowing the sun's full intensity to strike the ground. It is why Palm Springs became synonymous with both the winter tan and skin cancer. Cacti indigenous to this region have evolved to thrive in intense ultraviolet light, but even these struggle in the summer months here. Many permanent plants that demand full sun in normal atmosphere can suffer significant problems in direct low desert sun.

Prefabricated shade cloth panels provide excellent seasonal shade to protect plants and outdoor spaces.

The change of seasons alters the position of the sun in the sky. As it moves further south for the summer and then north again in the winter, the exposure of plants is varied. Container gardens make sense because they can be moved with the seasons to protect against midsummer sun damage and winter frost.

Plants react to excessive sun in different ways. Leaf scorch results in brown blotches or the crisping of leaf edges. With succulents, the plant becomes yellow under too much direct sun. This color may fade back to green as the seasons change. But when the exposure is just too great and permanent damage results, the yellow continues to discolor to brown, with ugly scabbing. For a beautiful green skin cactus or succulent euphorbia with few thorns, this can result in irreparable damage. Though unsightly, the best temporary seasonal protection is to drape shade cloth over the exposed part of the plant for the summer. Shade cloth is sold by the yard in varying densities at most home improvement stores.

MO TIPS

Beware of long-lived perennials tagged for full sun. In the Coachella Valley they may do well the first winter but are unlikely to survive the summer to bloom again the following year. Plant beneath winter pruned trees that allow sunlight penetration for the cooler months, then allow the trees to grow dense again for the summer to protect perennials in the heat.

Modern style homes utilize semi-transparent panels as fences and windbreakers without sacrificing light.

WIND

The wind farm at the west end of the Coachella Valley attests to the epic winds experienced here. The old tamarisk tree windbreaks were planted to reduce its effects and that of blowing sand so severe, it can pit automobile glass. It is difficult for even desert-adapted plants to survive these conditions.

In some seasons, typically spring and fall, high winds cause broken branches and blow-over of trees. Just take a look at the trees in Desert Hot Springs to see how wind can spoil their form and thin foliage. Even tough palms and moisture holding succulents have a hard time there, and those that manage to survive lose their natural beauty.

The biggest challenge of wind is desiccation. This is the drawing of moisture out of the leaves of a plant through tiny pores known as stomates. Plants that evolved in arid regions around the world have natural defenses against wind borne moisture loss. Try to grow plants from more humid climates and they'll instantly wither.

When the rate of moisture loss becomes greater than the rate at which the roots can replace it, leaves die. Few new ones form. This makes it nearly impossible to get a young tree started because it is water-starved from day one. Older trees may leaf out in calm periods only to be stripped again by wind. Many of the newer developments down the center of the valley are seeing the effects of this on their young landscaping. The plants grow so desiccated they are stunted even at maturity.

Outside the extreme wind belts, wind damage can still destroy a beautiful tree. Many desert adapted species can be weak limbed and suffer significant breakage in ordinary windy desert conditions. This is a hazard to people, structures, and automobiles. However, if the overall volume of the canopy is thinned out, reducing wind resistance, breakage is far less likely and blow-over reduced. The remaining branches tend to become stronger too. Do not confuse thinning with topping which is further described in chapter 9—"The Trees". Thinning is beneficial to the tree; topping destroys its natural beauty and can actually encourage more undesirable rank growth later on.

Nestled against the wash, the old Neil's Nursery, later renamed Palapas, was the heart of the Palm Springs gardening community for decades.

HEAT

Even if you leave the valley for the summers, your garden doesn't. Every plant that is to remain behind must be tolerant of the summer here. Next to Death Valley, the Coachella Valley summer is the hottest in the United States.

Do not confuse heat with solar exposure. Heat occurs whether a plant is in full shade or sun, under cover, or out in the open. It is the ambient air temperature that can reach staggering levels in July through September.

Many plants that are suited to warm climates may not be able to tolerate these temperatures even under the best conditions. This is why you never see certain plants in valley landscapes that hail from warm climates elsewhere.

For example, New Zealand Flax, a very popular plant for droughty gardens and landscaping along Los Angeles freeways, thrive west of Banning. But try to grow them in the valley and they literally melt down. Meltdown is a common term to describe how a plant collapses from the heat. The cells that make up its structure literally disintegrate and the plant is lost. No amount of care, relocation, or water will save it. This reaction is purely genetic and indicates the plant simply won't grow in our climate.

Sometimes nursery plants grown in coastal nurseries and brought into the valley to be sold will exhibit the very same characteristics. This meltdown may not be genetic, but a reaction to suddenly being forced into such a blistering climate. Their stomates are much larger to allow for greater transpiration rates on the mild coast. When they come here, too much moisture is lost through the stomates and the plant withers. Sometimes it will die back to the stem or root, but don't be in a hurry to dig it out. This remnant may regrow next year. But this second grow-out will bear smaller leaves with more efficient stomata. Often foliage may itself appear more streamlined or sparsely held. That's how plants adapt to changes in their climate and that too is in the genes.

WATER AS A HEAT CONDUCTOR

During the depths of the summer the soil surface layer becomes blistering hot by the end of the day. If you water in the early evening before the soil has cooled, you risk damage to plant roots. Water applied to the hot surface picks up heat, then acts as a conductor carrying it deeper into the soil. Sudden exposure to hot water can burn roots that otherwise would be protected deeper down. To avoid this problem wait until very late in the day to water, after surface temperatures have cooled, or do so early in the morning.

To successfully cultivate any succulent plant, whether in ground or in a pot, ensure the soil is extremely fast draining. Drainage may require a large percentage of sharp sand and gravel to provide avenues for water to pass through. Beware of bagged topsoil and potting soil because these are not sufficiently well drained for most succulents and cacti.

SOIL

In ancient times the Coachella Valley was once an inland sea. It was named after the Spanish word for shell, and you can still find small seashells in some soils here. The soil is noticeably lacking in organic matter, so its fertility tends to be limited in the west end of the valley. In more recent history just a few centuries ago, a great lake lay at the east end of the valley and was ringed by extensive marshland that drew Native Americans from all directions to hunt water fowl and to fish. This is why soils around Indio are so fertile they support extensive agriculture.

Soils in the Palm Springs and Desert Hot Springs are influenced by the windy pass and tend to be heavy with sand. The same is true down the wind belt of Thousand Palms and Bermuda Dunes. Drainage is expressed and there is little nutrition for plants not adapted to a Spartan diet. However, these can be some of the best soils for gardening because we can augment them with bagged compost and fertilizers, both organic and synthetic. Sandy soils will dry out very quickly, so it is essential to water often to keep plants adequately hydrated in the summer months. This is doubly important in the wind belt communities.

Around the foothills that edge the valley which include the coves of La Quinta, Palm Desert, Cathedral City, and south Palm Springs including the Mesa, soils can be more challenging. They are rocky and the earth can reach the consistency of concrete with only slightly greater fertility than the sand. Some of these hardpans exposed to water experience natural cementation due to minerals which set up much like concrete. This cementation can restrict drainage so that water applied runs off before it is absorbed slowly into the soil. Therefore irrigation must be carefully designed to mitigate this poor drainage and maximize its effectiveness with much slower applications.

For these soils, the best way to improve conditions is the healthy addition of finely ground compost. Organic matter interferes with the natural cementation, keeping soil particles from packing so tightly together. These larger gaps allow water, fertilizer, and plant roots to penetrate more efficiently. Compost also provides food for soil microorganisms that render a soil more biotically rich and beneficial to plants.

WATER

Water is the desert's most precious resource, and sadly it is too often exploited in our valley. Lawns and golf courses are the major offenders that require incredible amounts of irrigation to survive here. For this reason we've left turf grass out of this book to encourage everyone to reconsider whether lawns are truly an efficient use of our limited natural resources.

The best way to water in the desert is to supply water to a plant and nowhere else. Not only does this reduce weed growth and maintenance in the desert landscape, it makes your plants far more healthy. Their water demands in the hot months are greater than traditional spray systems can provide. But there is another reason why spray systems can be a problem.

Plants root only where there is water. When a spray system covers large areas with airborne spray, the water you apply must reach a huge area of ground. The moisture penetrates only a few inches deep, which is adequate until the next watering time in the cycle. The plants will concentrate their roots in that shallow layer to capture as much moisture as they can. But come summer and the surface temperature of the soil skyrockets. This water grows less abundant and the roots are subjected to the full force of surface soil heat. Without the ability to root for deeper hidden moisture, they fail to do well and may die if there is a sudden heat wave.

Spray systems can also have big problems in windy climates. New homes in the wind belt will suffer the most from water drifting out of its designated location in gusty weather. Stream heads were designed to water better under these conditions, but even these can be challenged by desert conditions. Plus, they still don't solve the shallow watering problem.

The sight and sound of water, as well as its importance to plant life, is more vital in the desert garden than any other landscape.

The key to creating your own new and interesting combinations of desert plants is grouping together those plants that demand the same water requirements, despite where they come from. Here the *Agave desmiettiana*, *Aloe eru*, and *Aloe ferox* all thrive equally well on the same sprinkler head. Drier plants such as the pink flowered native *Opuntia basiliaris* on page 7 or *Aloe dicotoma* would quickly rot and die under these very same conditions.

The key to success is to think about flooding the root zone with water. This was traditionally done with a bubbler head on a standard riser that supported one tree or shrub. They emit a great deal of water and one or two can support a sizeable tree. The water pools around the base of the tree to gradually percolate down to a greater depth than spray. When the surface soil heats up and dries out, there will be plenty of water deeper down, so roots naturally seek it out. Bubbler grown trees, shrubs, and vines are much more vigorous and resistant to periodic drought than those watered strictly with spray heads.

The advent of microirrigation in Israel led to a whole new way of watering our desert landscaping. Microsystems operate on lower pressure than a standard system, which means there's less pressure at the joints, allowing parts to connect without special glues. This low pressure system utilizes the same idea as the traditional desert high pressure bubbler system which allowed one heavy flow head per plant. With low pressure systems, emitters replace the heads with at least one for each plant in the landscape. Unlike flooding bubblers, microsystems deliver very slowly to a single location where it percolates down deep into the soil encouraging roots to seek it there.

For some plants like annuals and groundcovers that are naturally more shallow rooted, or where we must cover many smaller plants in a condensed area, pin point emitters aren't suitable. Instead a microspray emitter sits upon a small plastic riser and sprays an area about a foot in diameter. It remains low flow and does so at a slower rate so they can water deeply but still keep the surface evenly moist.

The down side to microirrigation is that it can be compromised in so many ways that it becomes a real problem for seasonal residents. Algae, minerals, bugs, and rodents can cause the hidden drip emitters to clog up. The thin spaghetti tubing can also become UV damaged and brittle, resulting in cracks and leaks that go unseen for long periods. These breaks deny water to heads at the end of the line, compromising a great deal of planting.

Unless the emitters are checked often, you may not realize there's a problem until the plant becomes so stressed it stands out from the others. By this time its beauty and health may be spoiled. With microspray systems the spray is easier to visually spot check, but these too are vulnerable to tubing leaks which can reduce overall water pressure.

FALL — SEPTEMBER 21 TO DECEMBER 21
START OF THE SEASON

The onset of this period depends largely on late summer humidity and nighttime temperatures.

- All annual color should be in the ground by the middle of October while soils are still warm enough to encourage fast root growth.

- Slow watering of Bermuda grass lawns, overseed with ryegrass.

- Prepare soil for vegetable and seasonal herb gardens by fortifying it with plentiful compost and manures. These contain nutrients as well as their own microorganism populations for healthy organic gardens. Unimproved desert soils can be woefully lacking in organic matter, which in turn reduces microorganism populations and water holding capacity.

- Adjust automatic watering schedule as days grow short and nights cool.

- Cut back water to all succulents to prevent possible rot from saturated soils deeper down in cooler temperatures.

- In some years, frosty nights can appear by the holidays, so be aware of the location of more frost-tender plants. If they are in pots, relocate them to places under patio covers or tree canopies that are warmer than surrounding open spaces. If you have larger frost-tender plants in the ground, keep a sheet handy to throw over them at night in anticipation of a cold snap.

WINTER — DECEMBER 21 TO MARCH 21
SPRING EQUINOX

- Bare root and container grown plants should be in the ground by the end of January.

- Make New Years Day your cue to plant leaf crops such as lettuce, and the cold loving kale, collards, and other greens.

- Early in this quarter you can dig up and divide your succulent plants.

- In preparation for spring winds, check and evaluate all staked trees to be sure the connections are solid and not causing girdling or damage to the bark. Deep water trees with a slowly dripping hose to send water to the entire root zone to draw upon in the coming growth period.

- As temperatures begin to warm it's time to fertilize citrus for their coming bloom season.

- Keep a sharp eye out for weeds that propagate rapidly as the days grow longer.

- If temperatures are warm enough by late February, plant tomatoes and peppers as well as other warm season vegetables.

- Keep an eye out for aphids, scale insects, and other garden pests as temperatures warm.

 ## THIS CHAPTER
IN A NUTSHELL

(1) The low desert experiences very high UV light levels that can burn plant leaves in the summer. Many plants will require shade or must be moved into shaded locations to protect against the worst of the summer weather.

(2) Nursery plants labeled for "full sun" elsewhere may require some shade throughout the day and full shade in the afternoon to survive the summer here.

(3) In some areas of persistent dry wind such as Desert Hot Springs, moisture can be drawn out of plant leaves faster than it can be replenished. Even supplemental watering will not be enough to prevent leaf death.

(4) Some plants cannot take the heat of the desert, even when in full shade.

(5) The best time of year to plant in the desert is in the fall to allow at least six months for plants to become established before high heat of summer begins.

CHAPTER 2

THE PALMS

View Palm Springs or Palm Desert from high points in the valley and all you see is a sea of palms. It's our desert's signature plant. These wild palms of the Coachella Valley are unique because they live in very few places on earth. Most are found in isolated water sources around the valley, foothills, fault lines, and dry washes. But still more can be found further south in similar far-flung oases. They are tiny remnants of primordial groves that once spread over much of southern California.

All other palms seen here are imports. The first to arrive was the date palm, an agricultural crop counted among the world's most ancient cultivated species. The east end of the valley was once famous for its date orchards, many of which have now been developed. From these orchards came the mature date palms transplanted into local development landscaping.

TELL TALE PALMS

To the uninitiated, all palms look alike. To those in the know, there are two fundamental differences that are easy for the newcomer to discern. All palms bear fronds, which are giant leaves on very thick stems known as petioles. The shape of the leaf can be round like a fan or long like a feather. Thus, a palm is grouped with either fan palms or feather palms. The natives are fan palms, and these bear a ball-shaped foliage head atop a thick straight trunk. Date palms are feather palms, formed with an umbrella-like head atop the trunk. There are types of both feather and fan palms that can also produce multiple trunks over time, such as the Mediterranean fan palm, *Chamerops humilis*. This different form is unique to smaller landscaping species.

OPPOSITE: The shaded floor of the Palm Canyon grove of *Washingtonia filifera*.

PALMS OF THE INDIAN CANYONS

The canyons just south of the city of Palm Springs are world famous for their oases of indigenous California fan palms, *Washingtonia filifera*. It is truly remarkable to look down from the Trading Post and see this isolated grove, and even more wonderful to walk the sandy floor of the oasis beneath their towering shade. It's no wonder the Cahuilla Indians consider these places their most precious heritage, strictly controlling entry and usage.

The Agua Caliente Band of Cahuilla Indians lived in the valley for aeons, thriving on the game and desert plants under the shelter of the native palm groves. They utilized nearly every part of these plants from the nutritious seeds to the trunks and fronds to make implements and dwellings. Historically the Cahuilla would set the groves on fire to burn away the accumulated skirts of the trees. This not only encouraged more seed production, it controlled pests and made it safer to live beneath the trees. Much of the litter accumulating in the palm canyons illustrates the value of burning, but now mechanical shredding helps to keep the trails accessible.

Palm Canyon is open to visitors every day. It is accessed by following Palm Canyon Boulevard south along the mountain into the canyon. At the gate to the Indian lands you must pay an entry fee. The groves are closed after dark.

INDIO DATE PALM GROVES

California fan palms bear large annual crops of nutritious black seeds.

Long before the desert became a resort playground, farmers found that the climate and soils around Indio were ideal for cultivation of the date palm. It is said that the date palm likes its feet in the water and its head in the fire, illustrating how much water they require to thrive and produce fruit. The date palm is dioecious—which means fruit-bearing trees are female, and pollen is borne only on male trees.

The USDA began a date growing experiment near Mecca, California in 1904 due to the locally abundant water supply. North African varieties were imported and planted with great success. By 1913 there were eight growers in the Indio area and the valley was on its way to worldwide recognition as a premier date growing region. Today the groves produce millions of pounds of dates each year. The date industry is not as strong as it once was, however, and many of the old groves that are no longer productive have been

transplanted to new locations around the valley. During the year these landscape trees still produce fruit, which is beautiful and attractive to birds, but not always desirable in the home garden.

UNDERSTANDING HOW PALMS GROW

The palm is unique in the world of trees. Most trees produce a thin cambium layer beneath their bark where water and nutrients flow connecting root to leaves. Wherever the cambium is cut, this vital flow ceases. But the palm has no cambium whatsoever. Its anatomy is so unique it's more like the stem of a grass plant than a tree.

The center of a palm trunk is packed solid with fleshy tubes that are each independent so the trunk can flex under high winds without breaking. The tubes are quite succulent and capable of holding a great deal of water for long periods of time. They are bound by an outer bark skin that protects them from damage and sunburn.

This internal moisture is made available to the central growing point of the foliage head as it is needed to continually produce new leaves. When fully hydrated, a massive amount of water is held in these tubes. This makes palms incredibly heavy and quite capable of withstanding prolonged drought without losing foliage.

ABOVE LEFT: Many of the Indio date groves were planted early in the twentieth century from plants shipped from North Africa. Photo credit: USDA

ABOVE RIGHT: Ripening date clusters are protected from birds and sunburn with brown paper covers.

Wild palms grow in the saturated streambed proving just how much water they can tolerate in the root zone.

WATER

Like cacti and other succulent plants, palms have roots that are capable of rapid water uptake. The foliage head is designed to catch rain and funnel it downward into the root zone. This rapid absorption helps to utilize water passing quickly through sandy soils or flash flooding down a wash. It's also perfect to catch what rain falls in late summer thunderstorms. Periodic flooding of young landscape palms during the heat of summer mimics the natural water cycle. It can be very effective at encouraging more rapid growth. It's also helpful at discouraging rooting at the surface of the soil which can interfere with other landscape plants. However, it is virtually impossible to overwater a palm when it's in well-drained sandy soils. The more common problem is with sluggish palm growth and browning of fronds due to overly dry conditions.

FEED

Palms are like grasses in another way too—they are strictly foliage plants. Sure palms flower and fruit, but that's often more a liability than a benefit. The nutrient responsible for leaf and stem growth, and the primary one in lawn fertilizer are the same. Nitrogen is the primary need of the palm, and adding supplements (provided there is adequate water in the summer), can have a big impact on growth. Some palms that demand more nitrogen than our native varieties can suffer deficiency in our sandy soils.

Tree spikes are the easiest way to slow feed your specialty palms during the fast growing season in the heat of the summer. Even if you leave for the off-season, spikes remain in place to slow release throughout the hot months.

These big compressed fertilizer spikes aren't designated for palms, so just select the ones with the highest dose of nitrogen. For record growth, replace them each season. Pound them into the soil at regular intervals at least a foot, preferably further out from the base of the trunk. You can replace the spikes in spring and fall, or do so each season four times a year for even faster growth. Just be sure there is enough water supplied to ensure they dissolve into the root zone.

PRUNE

After a high wind you'll find chunks of fan palm fronds and flower stalks scattered throughout the streets in desert communities. There's no question they present a serious hazard to people, vehicles, and even structures. It's a matter of safety that the palms are pruned, but not all palms need this care. The tall, thin Mexican fan palms are the major offenders because they readily release dead fronds. The native California fan palms hold their skirts on, which can be seen on Palm Canyon street trees and those in the Indian Canyons. However, they do shed the huge woody stalks that formerly bore flowers and seed, and these are annually removed by the city.

Pruning palms has become a major industry in the Coachella Valley. It is not essential to the health of the plant, but it is a good way to keep palm seed from populating your yard with millions of quick-to-germinate sprouts. It also eliminates flying stalks and helps to keep the trunk of a palm evenly latticed with petiole bases. For a price, professional palm pruners will also strip the old petioles off a palm to reveal a beautiful smooth trunk.

There has been an alarming trend to overprune palms. The thinking is that the more they cut the less they must do next time. However, when too much is removed the central meristematic tissues are overly exposed to sun and dryness. They haven't had a chance to develop a tougher skin against the sun, and it also makes them vulnerable to entry by insect parasites. Moisture loss, sunburn, and wind damage can reduce the health of the palm because loss of enough meristematic tissue can kill the "heart."

TRANSPLANT

Many palms sold today are adults. They may be dug from the growing grounds with heavy equipment and transported to be replanted at a new location. You can go to the growing grounds and hand-pick your trees if the grower is willing. The cost is usually based on the trunk-foot measurement, which is the number of feet of trunk from the top of the root ball to the base of the foliage head. Use trunk-foot prices to shop suppliers to get the best deal. Also note if the petiole bases have been stripped off because a clean trunk palm will cost significantly more per trunk-foot than a lattice

Date palms were planted to shade this early Movie Colony home. Because palms retain so much water in their trunk, only a small root ball need be taken when transplanting. The fronds are tied up to make them easier to move, but more importantly to protect the heart of the foliage head inside for many weeks after transplanting until new roots are capable of replacing lost moisture. Less leaf surface exposed to the sun reduces photosynthesis, a process which requires a good deal of water.

TOP: The roots of the palm will be flooded regularly after the fronds are untied.

BOTTOM: The uniformity of growth and thick trunks clearly distinguishes the California fan palm street trees from the tall Mexican palm at far left.

trunk. While this is the most expensive choice, it is the best way to obtain instant shade or large scale drama for a newly landscaped site.

Larger palms can be grown in big wood boxes, which also require heavy equipment to move, but since they may not be as old as the field-grown plants, these costs will be lower. Rare palms are often grown this way and may only be obtained as boxed specimens. Due to ease of transport, they may also have been grown closer to the coast, and can have difficulty adapting to sudden changes in conditions. Before making a selection, be sure they have been in the desert at least a year for full acclimatization.

The least expensive way to obtain palms is to buy them in 15-gallon pots, then once in the new location provide plenty of water and fertilizer to speed growth. This kind of care can save you thousands of dollars in plant costs.

PALMS FOR PALM SPRINGS

It may seem that selecting palms to grow in the Coachella Valley is a no-brainer, but that's not necessarily true. Each kind of palm has its place in the landscape, and some are far more vulnerable to drought and wind damage than others. A few are even *plantas non gratas* here. Knowing the difference can not only save you money, it guarantees lush healthy palms to shade and beautify your home.

NATIVE FAN PALMS
AND THEIR MEXICAN COUSINS

The palms that define the Coachella Valley and much of southern California are nearly identical in youth to another closely related species. However, you'll easily see the differences if you come into Palm Springs on Highway 111 and cruise down Palm Canyon Drive. The thick skirted native *Washingtonia filiferas* are occasionally broken by a few tall, skinny individuals that tower over their companions. Those nonconformists are *Washingtonia robusta*, the Mexican species found in northern Mexico and Baja California. They were probably planted by mistake when they were young.

This illustrates how important it is to ensure your palms are of pure species and well marked when purchased as babies in nursery containers. This is doubly important for landscape design where uniformity of growth is paramount. To complicate matters, the California and Mexican fan palms can cross pollinate, and their seed produces trees with unpredictable size and form.

Washingtonia filifera | **California Fan Palm** | 60 feet tall | Full Sun | Single Trunk | This is the palm indigenous to the Coachella Valley that bears large fronds up to 6 feet across. Fronds are retained on the thick trunk to create a skirt of dead foliage. Trees bloom in spring with showy inflorences 8 to 10 feet long. Palm flowers are pollinated by wind, then attractive clusters of black seed dangle from the stalks until consumed by birds.

Washingtonia robusta | **Mexican Fan Palm** | 100 feet tall | Full Sun | Single Trunk | The tall, lanky native of Mexico is fast growing, bears smaller fronds, and a less majestic foliage head. Dead fronds will be held for a time, but in high winds they easily detach. This problem of flying away in high winds has led to the widespread trimming of palm skirts. This palm is significantly cheaper to buy than its California cousin. Growth can be so much faster that the foliage head soon rises out of sight and presents a serious problem of accessibility for annual pruning.

Washingtonia robusta

Arecastrum romanzoffianum | **Queen Palm** | 30 feet tall | Full sun | Single Trunk | This is the most feminine of all our desert palms. Feather fronds bearing distinctive crinkled leaflets contribute an ostrich-feather look to the foliage heads. Better adapted to more humid climates, they crave plentiful regular watering in the desert. It fares well when the root zone is shaded by other plants so surface temperatures of the soil don't stimulate so much evaporation. This palm is less tolerant of wind than fan or date palms. Brown fronds often plague specimens not adequately watered and fed. It may be impossible to cultivate in the wind belt.

Arecastrum romanzoffianum

RESPECT THE PHOENIX PALM QUARANTINE

Date palms are vulnerable to a serious fungus known as *Fusarium oxysporum* or Fusarium Wilt. It can be spread by other closely related palms from the genus *Phoenix*. These include the Canary Island Date Palm (*Phoenix canariensis*), the Senegal Date Palm (*Phoenix reclinata*), and the Pygmy Date Palm (*Phoenix robelenii*). Though quite common in Los Angeles and San Diego, these palms are technically illegal to bring into the Coachella Valley. The risk of carrying fusarium in their soil and fleshy tissues is just too great. While San Diego County is a major growing ground for *Phoenix* palms of all kinds, these populations grown outside the valley should not be brought into our area either by residents or professional landscapers.

RIGHT: *Chamerops humilis*

Chamerops humilis | **Mediterranean Fan Palm** | 10 to 20 feet tall | Morning sun or part shade | Multiple Trunk | This is the best short palm for landscaping and the most expensive due to slow growth. It begins as a single trunk that produces offsets at the base that develop into secondary trunks with their own foliage head. This is a very cold tolerant species and considered highly attractive, particularly under night lighting. Older boxed multiple trunk specimens can be very pricey. This is a preferred specimen for use around swimming pools due to its strong architectural form and slow growth. It offers a decidedly North African look to Moroccan themes and traditional Spanish architecture.

Trachycarpus fortunei | **Windmill Palm** | 10 to 30 feet tall | Part shade | Single Trunk | This small, single trunk fan palm from Asia is often confused with the Mediterranean fan palm. Consider the windmill a pint-sized version of the California fan palm, with the addition of a fuzzy, fibrous trunk. It is less resistant to dry wind and direct sun here in the desert, which relegates it to protected spaces among buildings, courtyards, and in sheltered gardens. This palm is an ideal candidate for containers, particularly in spare modern boxes and cylinders that rely on its symmetry for drama.

Phoenix dactylifera | **Date Palm** | 60 feet tall | Full Sun | Single Trunk

The majority of date palms in valley landscapes have been moved from the old orchards. Occasional smaller specimens can be found at homesites, but their size and the great diameter of the foliage head can be too large for a city lot. Dates produced on the female forms can be a litter problem, as are the birds that devour them. However, this is also a benefit for wildlife lovers. Occasionally a shrubby, multiple trunk male date palm will appear in old neighborhoods. These make excellent impenetrable privacy hedges for larger sites due to their dense foliage and tendency to sucker.

THE CYCADS

Long before palms evolved, cycads ruled the earth. These very primitive palm-like plants are related to pines and other conifers, even though they look like palms. This is proven by how they reproduce. Mature specimens produce cones at the center of their foliage head that look and act just like pine cones for reproduction.

Many cycad species resemble large ferns, and therefore can be used to give fern-like looks to desert gardens that need the same lush effect. Their stiff evergreen foliage and ability to withstand extreme heat makes them a great choice for the low desert. Since the family of cycads includes genera from around the world, not all of them will grow here. There is an excellent collection in the Living Fossil Garden at the Living Desert. While only a few are commercially available in the valley, it is likely that a good number of others just haven't been tested here yet. Due to slow growth, it takes a great deal of time to test these plants in our climate.

It's best to treat cycads in the landscape as you would a small, ground-dwelling palm. They are exceptional in sheltered locations. All over the valley some very large, old cycads can be found on the north sides of buildings and in enclosed courtyards where direct sun is rare. The common sago palm (*Cycas revoluta*) thrives here provided it is not exposed to direct sun in the summer months. It provides a sense of green lushness and architectural form for locations where more traditional plants dry out. All cycads do well in ground or in pots that can be moved around with the seasons for optimal exposure.

Phoenix dactylifera

A very old specimen cycad can develop multiple trunks and reach tree-like proportions.

Cycas revoluta. With age the cycad may develop its exotic central cone.

The long, fern-like leaves of *Dioon spinulosum* contrast sharply against the wide rounded leaves of *Zamia furfuracea*, both reliable desert cycads.

Fortunately, interest in cycads over the last few decades has resulted in the presence of many growers throughout San Diego County. These specialists have made many of the formerly rare cycads available to the wholesale market, and subsequently they appear at garden centers. It is difficult to know exactly how each cycad will do in the valley, but if the location is suitable nearly all should thrive.

Typically cycads have been the darlings of the modern style because they are so strongly architectural. But remember, they are chameleons which can change character according to their surroundings and companion plants. Whether grown as a single specimen in a truly stellar container or grouped into a shaded patio space to offer the tropical look, the cycad rarely disappoints. After all, a plant that has changed little in three hundred million years has got to be incredibly resilient.

Cycas revoluta | **Sago Palm** | The long-cultivated sago palm is a misnomer as it's not a palm. It's been used in Palm Springs gardens for decades, its precise symmetrical form favored for modern architecture. This is a slow-growing cycad and thus very expensive with large specimens costing thousands of dollars.

Most cycads are grown outside the valley so these plants will need shade throughout the summer. If overexposed, their beautiful foliage becomes yellow with scorch, then brown. They are very slow to recover. Reserve these plants for sheltered courtyards and beneath protective canopies of shade trees and structures.

Dioon spinulosum | This is the best cycad for creating fern-like looks in the desert. Though it appears luxuriant and soft, the bright green leaves are in fact tough and sharply pointed, reaching 6 feet long. Reliable and litter free, this is a most promising species for desert landscapes beneath protective shade trees. A native of southeast Mexico, it is surprisingly heat tolerant.

Zamia furfuracea | This is a unique cycad from Veracruz that thrives in desert heat offering a superior plant for patio pots or in ground. Its leaves are wide and backed by a russet colored fuzz giving them more color than other cycads. Long, graceful fronds are open and transparent, providing an airy look. Plants can tolerate more direct sun than other cycads during the winter months. Protect from frost.

MODERN JURASSIC

Equisetum hyemale | **Horsetail Reed**

Much larger ancestors of this primitive reed dominated the landscape of the dinosaurs. Today it's favored by modern designers for uniformity of growth, which create bold graphic effects. Segmented like bamboo, each rod is about the diameter of a pencil. Underground roots spread into dense colonies of super straight, bright green stems that grow ultradense with time. They are a fine problem solver for narrow slots in pavement. Try them for outstanding effects in pots. Equisetum take on better coloring and stiffer rods if well watered. They're naturalistic if allowed to grow unhindered, or can be topped to any height to create rigid blocks of green rods in the landscape.

LOCATION: SHIELDS DATE GARDEN

There is no better place to learn about the palm than at Shields Date Garden in Indio. These age-old groves of date palms were planted in the 1920s, after the USDA's experimental efforts proved the Coachella Valley was prime date palm territory. Floyd and Bess Shields were pioneer date farmers, tending their groves and lecturing on this fascinating, ancient crop. They prepared and sold the famous date shakes that tourists relished, particularly in the early years when the valley was still sparsely populated. Floyd Shields created a famous film, *Romance and Sex Life of the Date*, which can be seen at the gardens every day. But Floyd was also vital to expanding the American date industry, breeding his own varieties such as 'Blonde' and 'Brunette,' which remain exclusive to the family's orchards to this day. Shields' date orchards have always been grown without chemical fertilizers or pesticides—long before the value of organic farming became widely accepted. Visit Shields to tour the groves, visit their fabulous store, learn about date growing, and see the film.

Shields Date Garden

80-225 U.S. Highway 111 | Indio, CA 92201-6599

(800) 414-2555 | (760) 347-0996 | http://www.shieldsdategarden.com

THIS CHAPTER IN A NUTSHELL

1 The native fan palm, *Washingtonia filifera* is preferable over the Mexican fan palm, *Washingtonia robusta*, yet they are visually identical as juveniles.

2 Prune away flower stalks early on to prevent seeds, which will sprout all over the garden and stain paving.

3 Queen palms, *Arecastrum romanzoffianum*, retain their beautiful green fronds without browning edges if watered and fed generously year-round.

4 Encourage faster palm growth by inserting many fertilizer tree spikes into the ground for a more consistent diet, particularly very sandy and well-drained soil.

5 Palms of genus *Phoenix* cannot be brought into the Coachella Valley from other areas because they may carry disease that could threaten the date palm groves.

CHAPTER 3

THE AFRICANS

Because our summers are "Africa hot," it's no wonder so many plants from the southern end of that continent thrive here. Not only do temperatures in that region soar during the dry season, the land can go many months without rain, and so must its indigenous plants. Some of the world's driest deserts exist there, namely the Kalahari. In parts of this arid land that bumps into the west coastline, it never rains at all. Plants survive strictly on dew deposited by Atlantic Ocean fogs that can travel miles inland at night.

Many African plant groups bear such remarkable similarity to American desert natives that they are often mistaken for one another. This is because both groups evolved to weather the same challenges of heat, aridity, and browsing wildlife using the very same qualities, such as vicious spines or thorns and toxicity. It is called convergent evolution.

For example, the Africans feature a vast family of euphorbias that may appear identical to cacti but they are not related at all. From Madagascar, the alluadias are paralleled in America by the ocotillo. South African aloes bear such similarity to our American agaves that they can be tough to tell apart except when in bloom.

Succulent species that originate in central South Africa and into the Namibian Desert as well as the dry side of Madagascar are much better choices for desert gardens. They are naturally adapted to our "Africa hot" summer temperatures, but even these plants may require light shade during the furnace months of summer to avoid damage to their foliage and stems.

SUCCULENTS ELUSIVELY DEFINED

Exactly what is a succulent? It's a plant that contains specialized tissues that hold water. This stored water becomes available to the plant as needed, allowing it to continue growing independent of soil moisture for a period of time. It explains why many

OPPOSITE: The world famous African section of the Desert Garden at the Huntington Library and Botanical Gardens.

succulents have limited root systems. Some succulents develop a single swollen part of their stem, known as a caudex, where the water holding tissues are concentrated. Others may produce them as tubers among the roots, resembling a potato. In most, the entire plant itself is succulent, lacking any woody parts at all. The sheer diversity of plant forms with succulent anatomy makes it tough to use hard and fast rules that apply to all of them.

CHIEF SUCCULENT PROBLEMS

While succulent tissues help store water, they can also be a serious liability. Unique problems of succulents dictate how we grow them and what to look for when they're doing poorly.

ROT | This is the one great vulnerability shared by all succulents. The soft, moisture-laden tissues are bound by a skin that keeps fungus and bacteria separate from the sterile tissues. Once the skin is nicked or water damage sets in these pathogens move very quickly. Wounds open the door to rot-promoting organisms even when soil conditions are dry or well drained.

Once established, rot is tough to stop. That's why it's important to inspect succulents every day for the first sign of discoloration, perhaps yellow and darkening to brown. Softening may precede discoloration of the rotted tissue while surrounding areas remain solid. When rot is discovered you have only two choices: The first is to cut out the rotted areas until you reach undamaged tissue. This wound should heal over in dry air. If the rot is in the roots, remove the plant from the soil, shake all dirt off, and allow it to sit in the open air for days. Once it's stabilized, cut off all rotted parts to fresh healthy tissue and give it a few more days to callus off before you replant.

SCORCH | The intensity of the summer sun in the Coachella Valley cannot be underestimated. The dry desert air offers little to diffuse the UV exposure. Just as your skin becomes sunburned, blistered, and may even develop raw wounds, so will the skin of a succulent if not protected in the summer. A seriously scorched succulent can be permanently disfigured. In some cases the plant will have the opportunity to grow out of its scorched skin, but this can take years with slow-growing specimens.

Scorch can be temporary or permanent. During the transitional seasons of spring and fall as the sun is moving north or south, some plants may be exposed to sun for a short time and will scorch or yellow. Most of the time this short-term scorch ceases weeks later when the sun changes angle. The yellow parts may "green-up" again if tissues aren't too badly damaged.

HEAT MELTDOWN | Summer temperatures can be too much for many succulents even when in full shade and well watered. Many popular forms of *Aeonium, Echeveria, Sempervivum,* and *Sedum,* though happy in Los Angeles are intolerant of our average daily temperatures. No matter what you do they will either die, fail to thrive, or melt down altogether. Many consider these groups as "bedding succulents," using them like annuals in the desert for their single season of beauty.

FROST | Because succulents contain so much water they are vulnerable to frost damage. It will occur at the tips where the plant will develop discoloration a day or two after it is exposed. While frost damage isn't dangerous per se, it does act like other wounds to allow rot to set into internal succulent tissues. Rain or sprinkler water applied during frost events, or introduced to these frost damaged spots, no matter how small, can instigate a more tenacious, fast spreading rot.

IN GROUND — IN POT

African succulents belong in desert landscapes. They are ideal for water conservation and offer a huge range of colors, forms, and textures. In the larger landscape, specimen succulents make a significant visual statement.

The primary criteria for success with succulents are summer shade and well-drained soil. Summer shade, be it from structures or tree canopies prevents sunscald. Plants on north or south sides of buildings also do better. Those on the east or west exposures receive unremitting sun in morning or blistering afternoons.

A vast number of smaller African genera are favorite plants for potted gardens. While they will grow in ground and are great for jewel gardens, they require a good deal of care to keep them properly watered, weeded, and shaded.

Potting lets you to move your succulents around with the seasons. During much of the year they may be set out in full sun to enjoy around the garden. When summer hits you can move them all into a protected location until temperatures drop in autumn and the sun angle changes. When ganged together in the shade it's much easier to keep them all adequately watered as well.

As succulents, these plants do not need large pots like other traditional plants do. An overly deep soil mass is likely to trap moisture that can lead to drainage problems and the potential for root rot. That is why they are often grown in shallow dishes, pans, bowls, or bonsai pots. Like bonsai pots, any containers with abnormally large drain holes are best. Small holes are too easily clogged with woody matter, roots, and mineral buildup.

MO TIPS

Use an inverted pot shard to cover the hole in the bottom of a pot. This keeps soil from filtering out while ensuring the drain hole never becomes blocked.

Bold succulents such as these *Echeverias* and *Sanseverias* make ideal seasonal color for winter gardens.

Soil mix should be specifically formulated for succulents to guarantee adequate drainage. Do not use native soil or sand because these can pack down into a hard impervious mass just as it does out in the desert. Sand also filters out of the drain hole when you water. Avoid reusing potting soil, particularly if it contained a plant that died. The soil may contain fungi or bacteria that can reinfect your new succulent. Before you reuse a pot, wash it out and scrub the surfaces, then dunk it in a 10% bleach solution for a few minutes to kill any residual organisms.

THE ALOES

Aloe vera is the most famous succulent on earth. It is just one of an incredible genus which contains over one hundred species, mostly from southern Africa. The rosette of foliage produces a fresh bloom stalk every year, sometimes many of them. This is the chief difference between aloes and agaves which bloom only once in a lifetime.

Bright red, orange, or yellow aloe blossoms are terrific hummingbird lures. Some smaller species bloom repeatedly, keeping the little birds in your garden throughout the year. Larger species are outstanding specimens in the garden, particularly under night lighting. Aloes can feature unique leaf colors with natural spotting and highlighted edges. Stress from seasonal change, heat, drought, and cold can cause some aloes to experience foliage color change from green to vivid reds.

Except for tough desert-grown *Aloe vera*, most aloes desire a sheltered location away from reflected pavement heat and hot afternoon sun. They thrive under a high canopy of palms or shade trees. Plants will do best in eastern morning light, but even then may require protection in the midst of summer.

Most aloes spread vegetatively by offsets, another similarity to agaves. Offsets are "pups" produced around the base of the parent plant allowing individuals to grow into significant colonies without seed. You can remove the offsets at any time to root new plants. This is a valuable quality because some aloes that grow very well here can be difficult to find for sale. Rooting offsets may be the best way to obtain more rare plants to create a fabulous garden for very little money.

The larger arborescent (tree) aloes rarely produce offsets. In the desert, *Aloe marlothii* and *Aloe dichotoma* can grow quite large if provided an ideal location. They are expensive to buy as specimens but make an incredible impact, particularly if used as an accent with mid-century modern architecture.

The moderate sized aloes which include *Aloe vera* offset freely like groundcover. These plants may be used in lieu of traditional woody shrubs for modern architecture. They also make prime single accents with boulders or rock outcroppings. Their size and prolific nature will keep you supplied with plenty of propagation opportunities to fill in the rest of the garden.

Small aloes are a treasure close up. They are excellent choices for dish gardens and as small potted accents. Collections of smaller aloes either in ground or in pots are charming because they repeat bloom. Long wiry stems are topped with some of the most delicate of all aloe blossoms that resemble traditional coral bells, a cool season perennial.

This collection of small "jewel box" aloes at the Huntington Botanical Gardens' greenhouse shows many of the species that grow outdoors here in high filtered shade.

⚠ ALOE CANCER

There is only one aloe disease which can afflict the leaves, stems, and even the flowers. Known as aloe blight or aloe cancer, it is easy to recognize. The growth becomes distorted into masses of tumor-like tissue which take on a gnarled, twisted form. It is caused by microscopic mites which cause infection, stimulating abnormal cancer-like cell growth. Unfortunately there is no cure and blight will spread to other aloes nearby. Because it's already in the plant's tissues, you can't treat it. Cutting off the affected parts will slow but not solve the problem. It only gives the mites that much more time to move on to undamaged plants. Simply throw away the entire plant and its associated pot in the garbage can. Sterilize any cutters or tools that come in contact with the plants in a 10% bleach solution.

A mature *Aloe dichotoma* will branch numerous times to develop a tree-like form with age.

Aloe marlothii

Aloe dichotoma | **Kokerboom tree aloe** | In central South Africa you will find this huge tree-sized aloe growing on the hills and ridges in an otherwise barren countryside. Its preference for high places indicates it's particular about drainage. The plant is named dichotoma for its unique forked branches. They do very well under our high, thin canopy desert trees that ensure its blue-green foliage remains blemish free. Plants struggle in full sun.

Aloe marlothii | *Aloe ferox* | **Tree aloe** | This is a big, ferocious-looking single trunk tree aloe. It produces a large blue tinted foliage head that may exceed 3 feet across at the widest point. Wickedly spiked leaf margins and small surface thorns give the leaves a striking appearance. When stressed this aloe will bring its leaves into the center like a closed daisy to reduce surface exposure to sunlight. As leaves age they color in pink and orange highlights. *A. marlothii* is renowned for its skirt of shriveled, bone-hard leaf remnants. The trunk may also be sheared clean for more architectural form. Plants bloom in spring with large antler-like stems at the top of the plant bearing gold blossoms tinged in red or orange. Note: This species is farmed in South Africa for aloe gel used in many cosmetics.

Aloe eru | Medium spreader | This aloe is distinguished by its dark green foliage and very long leaves that may curl a bit in larger specimens. Considered one of the best midsized aloes for landscaping, it becomes quickly established and begins offsetting at an early age. Plants flower in tall spikes with short branching at the tips which bear orange blooms, but their chief value is as a massed foliage plant. Tolerance for sun is high provided they are kept to east-facing exposures when planted against walls or fences.

Aloe striata aka *Aloe karasbergensis* | Medium clumper | When pinkish-gray *Aloe striata* is happy and full of water it is the most brittle succulent on earth. Sometimes the slightest pressure will cause a leaf to split, then it is spoiled permanently. Delicate to handle or transplant, the pale coloring and accent striping are well worth special handling. This aloe is quite sun sensitive but too much shade can discourage blooming. Its slightly tougher cousin, *A. karasbergensis,* shares similar coloring with pin striping running the length of the leaf.

Aloe vera | Medicine Aloe | This tough species was the first aloe to be brought into cultivation but its exact point of origin is unknown. Formerly known as *A. barbadensis*, it has been renamed *vera*, meaning "true" aloe. As a landscaping aloe for desert gardens, it is unsurpassed for tolerance of heat, drought, and direct sun. Under stress the normally pale green leaves will take on reddish tones, the clumps closing in on themselves for protection. This aloe produces really attractive large bright yellow bloom stalks that stand perfectly upright. *Aloe vera* is quick to offset, making them easy to find and propagate. However, propagation from a desert-grown mother plant, particularly one in a trying location, will yield sun-tolerant offspring. This is important because *Aloe vera's* tendency to cross pollinate with other aloes may produce less resilient offspring.

GREAT SMALL ALOES FOR GARDENS

The art of jewel box gardening is the use of smaller succulents in tight knit groups. Smaller aloes are perfect for desert gardens because they hold up under the heat, bloom long, and offer spectacular color. Haunt the succulent displays at home improvement stores to find these tiny aloes where they cost just a dollar or two.

Aloe eru bloom. The dark green aloe at far right produces branching stalks of apricot-orange blossoms.

FAR LEFT: *Aloe humilis* is commonly known as the hedgehog aloe which produces dense blue-green clumps sporting bright orange flowers.

ABOVE CENTER: *Aloe juvenna* is normally bright green, but under the right conditions foliage takes on a red coloring.

ABOVE RIGHT: *Aloe rauhii* is a flat leaf grass aloe which bears charming coral colored bell-shaped flowers.

MEDICINAL *ALOE VERA* Studies show that *Aloe vera* not only helps skin to heal, it's also antibacterial. When you cut an aloe leaf it exudes a mucilaginous substance—this part contains the medicine. It may be applied directly to the skin to treat virtually any kind of wound. Fresh aloe is particularly effective on sunburn, insect bites, and dermatitis caused by prickly pear glochids.

Euphorbia trunacali

At that price you can afford to start collecting them to study their unique forms, colors, and blossoms at close range. They won't be labeled, and you may never know their species, but that doesn't matter as long as they grow and bloom well.

Plant aloes directly into well-drained garden soil where there is bright shade to protect from afternoon sun. Small aloes multiply quickly after the first season and will begin blooming when quite young. You can buy larger potted aloes, but they can be expensive in quantity and in the end they all turn out the same. Smaller plants are also easier to tuck into pebble fields and pockets around garden boulders.

THE EUPHORBIAS

To the untrained eye, many euphorbias appear identical to cacti. Though often confused, the two groups are wholly unrelated. The chief difference is that euphorbias bear thorns and cacti have spines, two very different structures that evolved for the same purpose: protection. While cacti are spectacular bloomers, all but a few of the euphorbias bear small, almost insignificant flowers. Nick the skin of a cactus and it bleeds clear or green. Nick the skin of a euphorbia and it bleeds white. Milky latex *Euphorbia* sap is of legendary toxicity. Many species have been used as arrow poison by indigenous African tribes.

The genus *Euphorbia* includes a few standout landscape plants that have proven themselves in the Coachella Valley. Dozens of small dish garden species make excellent porch or patio plants too. Though not included here, these small forms are rarely labeled with botanical names due to the large amount of nearly identical species. The following euphorbias are good garden plants that can be found for sale at local garden centers. They reach large sizes for instant impact. Beware of those grown on the coast as they will need some time to acclimate. Those propagated here in the desert will be more adaptable, but still may be sensitive to direct afternoon sun.

Euphorbia tirucalli | **Pencil Tree** | Tree | This easy to recognize species of Madagascar features segments roughly the size of a pencil. Smooth and thornless plants grow quickly to reach tree-like proportions at maturity. The most popular form known as "firesticks" takes on vivid red-orange coloring in the winter. It achieves best color in full sun. Careful pruning and thinning can influence overall size and appearance. Easy to propagate from cuttings. Outstanding fine-textured form for January color when few desert plants are in bloom.

Euphorbia ingens | **Candelabra Euphorbia** | Tree | Called the candelabra euphorbia, its upright form produces a strong main trunk which branches freely. This plant is often sold in its cream colored variegated form. Branches feature pronounced ridges edged with small, stubby thorns. They make excellent subjects for sheltered gardens and courtyards as potted specimens that can be moved with the seasons. The variegated forms seem to be more sensitive to overwatering and heat.

Euphorbia milii | **Crown of Thorns** | Shrub | Crown of thorns, named for its spiky stems, is the most colorful of all euphorbias bearing striking red blossoms that are produced freely in season. The species, which came into cultivation early on due to its color, is a native of Madagascar. It's ideal for terra cotta pots to accent Spanish style architecture. New large leaf and flower *E. milii* forms may not share the heat or drought resistance of their ancestors. Grow on a porch or patio and in sheltered spots beneath trees or patio covers. They may become deciduous in midwinter.

Euphorbia grandicornis | **Cowhorn Euphorbia** | Shrub | This plant earned the name "cowhorn" from the large pairs of thorns that line the ridges of its stems. Much like *E. ingens* in form, this

---

MO TIPS

EUPHORBIA SAFETY

The latex in all *Euphorbia* species can cause serious skin irritation and will even produce blistering. The chief problem is when latex enters the eyes and nasal passages. This may not be a direct contamination, because bits of latex can travel into the eyes via perspiration on the forehead. If the latex is on your hands it is easily transferred to the eyes and other sensitive areas if you fail to wash directly after handling the plants. If you prune a larger plant, let the cuttings fall and finish the job another day when the sap has flowed and completely dried.

(1) Whenever you prune large Euphorbia, and in particular the sap rich *E. tirucalli*, the pencil tree, it's a good idea to wear protective eye goggles. The plants bleed so profusely that the slight flick of a stem or cutters can send this latex in your eye. The high degree of toxicity can be severely painful and may cause temporary, even permanent blindness.

(2) Clark Moorten of Moorten Botanical Garden tells us that the juice of a small succulent, *Aeonium lindleyi* has long been considered the ancient antidote to Euphorbia poisoning. It is safe to apply the Aeonium to skin rashes or blisters caused by Euphorbia latex. While it has in the past been used to mitigate eye damage it is not recommended nor proven for such use. This Aeonium is prone to die or melt down during the heat of the summer. To keep the antidote on hand, grow it in pots you can move indoors for the hottest months.

Euphorbia grandicornis

Euphorbia trigona

plant has more radical habit and three sided segments. It has a stronger tendency to branch lower down on the stem creating a shrubby shape that spreads up to 5 feet tall and wide at maturity. The blossoms on these ridges between thorn pairs are small but quite visible. They are an excellent alternative for traditional shrubs along foundations and fence lines where adequately protected. This plant may be grown in pots but it can become unwieldy. It is best grown in ground and pruned to stimulate stronger branching. Highly vulnerable to wind damage and sunburn.

Euphorbia trigona | **African Milk Tree** | Shrub | Unlike the large landscape euphorbias, this smaller version is a superior porch and patio choice. Very dense upright growth on nearly spineless branches produces a strong architectural choice for shaded locations. When grown beneath small gaps in overhead structures it will reach for the light with excellent symmetry. At maturity plants may reach 6 feet with dense branching for a striking columnar form. Look for cultivars with distinctive mottling and red coloration that may become more or less intense in winter. The plants are nearly always grown in pots due to marked intolerance of wet soil.

THE KALANCHOES

Easy and resilient, the kalanchoes are some of the most unique plants for desert gardens. Some can even become weedy where conditions are right. One form that thrives in the desert produces leaves edged with dozens of tiny pups designed to drop off and root around the mother plant. Once pups start falling, the plant can infest a garden where conditions are right. For this reason both large and small forms of *Kalanchoe daigremontiana*, though attractive and bright-blooming, can become a problem. Although a huge number of *Kalanchoe* species exist, only the two most adaptable are featured here. Both require significant shade in the summer, but each serves an entirely different role in the garden. Tall flower stalks are dramatic but not particularly colorful.

Kalanchoe beharensis | Cultivars and hybrids | This is a huge succulent that can reach over 8 feet tall here in the desert. It is characterized by large thick leaves coated with a dense grayish pubescence. Undersides of the leaves take on a russet-brown tone adding to its visual interest. The species is highly variable, with many different leaf shapes. This group develops large branching flower spikes at branch tips which share the same color as the rest of the plant. Mid-century breeders introduced cut leaf edges, bumps, some with ruffles, and still more varieties were for increased blooming. Their presence became hallmark of high post and beam mid-century home interiors. The species produces one or more thick woody trunks. Numerous thinner stems of the cultivars create a shrubbier plant. All are ready rooters wherever they contact earth.

Kalanchoe beharensis

Kalanchoe thyrsiflora | **Flapjacks** | Trendy jewel box succulent gardens feature these striking plants with their pancake-like brightly colored leaves. Consecutive blue-green leaves brighten to red on edges and back sides in direct winter sun. Plants are preferred in their tidy juvenile rosettes. With onset of summer these bolt or elongate into bright orange flower stalks, spoiling their unique geometry. After flowering, cut back to basal stems that will recover by producing a multitude of smaller rosettes. These may be detached and rooted into new plants. Flapjacks are typically grown in pots with *Echeverias* because both are ephemeral plants treated much like an annual to be replaced each year. Requires shade in summer. Coveted by designers for elaborate mixed succulent bowls. Equally suited to porch, patio, and indoor-outdoor spaces.

Kalanchoe thyrsiflora

OTHER AFRICANS

Portulacaria afra | **Elephant's Food** | Jade Tree | This tiny leaf jade tree of the desert is a refreshing relief from the often muted hues of desert plants. Willingness to grow despite rugged conditions makes this a first-class choice for gardens. Plants develop arching branches, becoming gracefully pendulous with age. Old plants that have suffered repeated pruning develop gnarled stems that are treasured as bonsai style specimens. They make outstanding sculptured potted accents at virtually any age. Stick a cutting into any moist pot of sand and it will take root in a matter of weeks.

Portulacaria afra

Alluadia procera | Alluadia is an African version of the ocotillo which rarely blooms and thus found limited popularity in the past. The key feature is its supple canes that branch and arch in a sexy array that is highly ornamental. Alluadia shadow patterns are most attractive cast upon simple stucco or plaster walls by low sun angles or creative night lighting. If tip-pruned they branch heavily into exotic forms. This species grows quickly in the heat when provided water, good drainage, and filtered summer shade. Rows of small leaves are a delight at close range when grown either in ground or in pots.

Stapelia gigantea | **Carrion Flower** | These ground hugging African succulents thrive in low desert sandy soils. A superior bloomer for shade, it is just one of a large group that evolved to attract flies as pollinators. With no honeybees in Africa these 10-inch-wide soft yellow blossoms emit a fetid odor that lures flies to lay their eggs and thus pollinate the flowers. Larvae hatch but do not survive. *S. gigantea* may be found locally in blood red or puss yellow flowering forms that are truly magnificent in ground or in pots. Little known but very well adapted, this desert lover owns the summer shade garden.

Pachypodium species | **Madagascar Palm** | Despite its common name, Pachypodiums are not palms but specially adapted succulents. Their fat trunks are for water storage and lined with wicked thorns to protect against browsing wildlife. Partly deciduous, the plants will lose some or all of their foliage in the winter. There are two species most often seen in shaded or sheltered desert gardens, but are most often grown in pots to move for protection from sun in summer and frost in winter.

The most common, *P. geayi* is the tallest and identified by its thin pinnate leaves. *P. lamerei* leaves are wider and lush, but produced less abundantly. It is the most commonly grown species due to its flowers, which are quite similar to the white oleander, a distant cousin. Both of these species will branch with time to produce fascinating specimens.

TOP: *Alluadia procera.*

CENTER: *Stapelia gigantea.*

BOTTOM: Tall *Pachypodium geayi* in the Madagascar Garden at the Living Desert.

POSITIVELY REPTILIAN HAWORTHIAS

This is a huge genus of very small succulents that share deep green bodies in a variety of forms. They are distinguished by surfaces rock hard to the touch or exceptionally smooth and transparent. The majority produce rosettes which sprout long, wire-thin stems topped with insignificant white flowers. Among these are mimicry plants such as *H. truncata* which appears more like a geological specimen than a plant. Due to their unique appearance and ease of cultivation, *Haworthia* is a favorite in bonsai pots and dish gardens for tabletops where they can be appreciated at close range.

Rigid *Haworthia truncata* features rectangular leaves which bear little windows on top through which sunlight penetrates to reach photosynthetic cells hidden deep inside.

In the desert, Haworthias can be grown in light shade where soils are adequately well drained.

This collection of *Haworthia* species in the greenhouse at the Huntington Library and Botanical Gardens in San Marino illustrates the fascinating range-forms within the genus and why they make such excellent potted specimens.

Shaped like an inverted flamingo head, gasterias are loaded with nectar that keep hummingbirds in the garden.

GASTERIA: BLEEDING HEARTS OF THE DESERT

Think of shade-loving Gasterias as a succulent form of the old time favorite woodland flower, bleeding heart, which is so popular further north. These tongue-leaf succulents are quite similar to Haworthias when not in bloom, but once they flower there's no mistaking a Gasteria. Little known and yet the most perfectly adapted African succulent to the Coachella Valley, this is one plant we should add to every homesite.

The clumps of leathery foliage produce tall, wiry stems decked out with dozens of unique dangling flowers shaped and colored like a flamingo head when those pink birds are nose down feeding on shrimp in the shallows. Hummingbirds find them irresistible.

Gasteria takes plenty of water in the summer (with good drainage!) and prefers drier winters. It is otherwise carefree. Grow them in ground, or in pots and dish gardens that you can move into high profile locations when they bloom, then relocate to the background for the rest of the year.

Where soil is sandy and well drained, grow Gasterias as a mass to compound their visibility and fill shaded corners with vivid color and hummingbirds.

LOCATION: THE DESERT GARDEN AT THE HUNTINGTON BOTANICAL GARDENS, SAN MARINO, CALIFORNIA

The Desert Garden at the Huntington is the world's best collection, just a short drive from the Coachella Valley.

The hallowed ground of cactus and succulent aficionados is not in the Coachella Valley, but just two hours east of us at the Huntington estate. The world-famous Huntington Desert Garden is a century-old ten acre landscape featuring the most complete collection of mature cacti and succulents in the world. The garden features not only natives of the American Southwest, Mexico, and South America, but it has also amassed nearly every important species from southern Africa and Madagascar.

What makes this such an important botanical venue is how the plants are laid out relative to one another. It's a treasure trove of ideas for growing succulents too often found in pots when they do perfectly well in the soil. With a climate more mild than our desert, many of the African plants grow to awesome sizes on this south facing hillside. It is a rare opportunity to see their characteristics first-hand in a quantity that can only be achieved over many generations of collecting and care. A visit in the late spring is a rite of passage for any desert plant lover. Discover the garden and pick up visitor information online at http://www.huntington.org

The Huntington Botanical Gardens
1151 Oxford Road
San Marino, CA 91108
(626) 405-2100

THIS CHAPTER IN A NUTSHELL

1. African Euphorbia species bleed toxic white sap that can cause serious damage to the eyes. Wash hands, face, and clothing immediately after pruning or handling these plants.

2. Fast-draining, sandy potting soil, and large drain holes in the bottom of a pot are essential to successful container gardening with African succulents.

3. All but a few aloes are vulnerable to leaf scorch if exposed in the summer months.

4. *Kalanchoes* and *Gasteria* are two little known, yet very desert hardy genera for modern gardens.

5. Jade tree, *Portulacaria afra* is the toughest and easiest to grow plant that can be pruned to create truly exotic, bonsai forms.

CHAPTER 4

THE CACTI

Cacti and the Coachella Valley seem synonymous, but it may surprise you to discover that only a handful of species grow wild on the valley floor. You'll find them far more abundant on the foothills and canyons. Close observation of their habitat proves they prefer certain places in which to grow. Boulders cast shade and trap moisture in the earth beneath them, so seedlings are more prevalent in rocky nooks and crannies. Young cacti are "nursed" by the shelter of larger woody plants such as creosote bush and desert willow. So there may be far more cacti around, they just aren't out in the open. Only when the nurse plant has died out or the cactus reaches sufficient height will you see a specimen in full sun. With maturity they will be far more capable of taking the desert sun.

Newcomers to the desert automatically assume that all cacti are equal. Truth is, the family of *Cactaceae* is in fact far more variable than you might imagine. There are species native as far north as Idaho and south as Argentina. Some adapted to below sea level deserts while others prefer equally dry conditions high in the Andes Mountains. Still more adapted to damp conditions of the tropical coast, which make them impossible to grow here. Moreover, within these climate zones they further adapt to various exposures from full sun to shady conditions sheltered by trees, mountainsides, and jungle cover. With such wide diversity, it's easy to see why so many cacti fail to grow well here.

Cylindropuntia bigelovii perched atop rocky cliffs above Andreas Canyon.

OPPOSITE: This barrel finally reaches above its brittle brush nurse plants.

41

MO TIPS

TEMPORARY SUN SHELTER

Whenever your cacti begin to show signs of sunburn, provide them with a temporary shelter for the summer months. Though not particularly attractive, simply lay a sheet of shade cloth over the top of a low cactus or drape it on a taller one. The spines keep the fabric up off the skin of the plant and may also help to anchor it in windy weather. Use twine to loosely wrap a specimen for the season.

Barrel cacti are among the most versatile landscape forms with varying size, color, and flowers.

To complicate matters further, where a cactus was grown can have a huge influence on its success. Northern San Diego County is one of the most prodigious commercial cactus growing regions in the world, and much of what comes into our garden centers originates there. Even though a cactus might be a species native to the Coachella Valley, if it's been raised in a much milder climate it will be ultrasensitive to local conditions. The plant will need to acclimate, requiring summer protection for a long time before its outer layers are sufficiently toughened to our hot, dry, UV intensive climate. It is always preferable to buy or take a cutting from a cactus that's been living in the Coachella Valley for years rather than choosing one of unknown origin.

SORTING OUT CACTI BY FORMS

The deeper you delve into the world of cacti the more complex it becomes. With so many genera and species, even the experts have trouble keeping them straight. The easiest way for home gardeners to sort out cacti is to first group them by growth habit and form. For example, a columnar cactus would be an ideal form to flank an entryway. Paddle cactus are wickedly sharp and fast growing, so these would be best kept well back from living areas. Small clumping types can be ideal for nestling into rocky outcroppings.

Be aware that many begin life as small round seedlings that can change their form significantly as they age. Often you won't know the true character of an unidentified seedling for many years.

BARREL | Barrel cacti are ball-shaped, but in old age they can elongate somewhat. Our native Ferocactus begins as a small spherical form but can become a fat column up to 5 feet tall in old age. Barrels can be treated as a single specimen or a small group. Golden barrels are a favorite in large colonies just like a groundcover.

COLUMNAR | This "fence post" form produces tall, narrow shapes like living architectural columns in the landscape. Some species such as "organpipes" produce multiple columns from a communal base. Others feature a single branching trunk. Columnar cacti are often planted as hedges such as the *Myrtillocactus* at Moorten Botanical Garden.

VINE | Cacti in tropical forest regions evolved to climb into trees and benefit from greater light and moisture beneath the canopy. Vine cacti are great for small spaces where they can be trained onto walls and fences or into trees for greater interest. Night blooming *Hylocereus* and rattails are our most successful types.

CLUMPING | Clumpers are ground-hugging species which produce many offsets around the original seedling. They can mature into dense mounds with many growth points. Each point produces its own set of flowers. Mammilaria and our native *Echinocereus* are among the most common clumps that make exceptional landscape plants.

PADDLE | The paddle stem cacti are mostly upright, outstanding plants. They behave much like shrubs in the dry landscape. They vary from ground-hugging mats to tree-sized specimens that produce plentiful blooms and fruit. Paddle cacti include our small native *Opuntia basilaris*, but most larger forms of unknown identification are sold by flower color and paddle qualities such as size, thorns, and skin color. Closely related to the paddles are "cigars" which include the entire cholla family including our native teddy bear cholla. They have recently been split off into a new genus, *Cylindropuntia*, to further distinguish them from the paddle stem *Opuntia*.

A fifty-year-old columnar *Pachycereus weberi*, native to Baja California.

Vine cacti may be small potted dangling forms, but those that do best in the Coachella are vigorous climbers treated like vines in the landscape.

Native California species of *Mammilaria* and *Echinocereus* both produce dense clumping forms.

Purple paddle prickly pear is one of the most colorful species.

MO TIPS

CACTUS FROM CUTTINGS

Columnar, vine, clumping, cigar and paddle cacti are among the easiest to root. Simply detach a piece from the mother plant at a natural joint. Allow the wound to dry out in a shady place for a few days. Once a dry callus has formed, insert the cutting into rooting medium. Our natural desert dune sand is an ideal rooting medium, but you can use other kinds of sand or cactus potting soil, or even plant directly into the ground.

COACHELLA VALLEY NATIVE CACTI

The best way to start gardening with cacti is to plant native species well adapted to local conditions. The best place to learn about them is in their natural habitat. Hike the Indian Canyons during spring bloom season. If you observe where they choose to grow and reproduce in the wild, you will know better how to position them for optimal performance in your garden.

Ferocactus cylindraceus | **Compass Barrel** | This large and extraordinarily beautiful barrel is native to the valley floor and the surrounding hillsides of Palm Springs. Overharvesting by locals for making cactus candy years ago decreased the valley floor population considerably. Today the oldest specimens are restricted to inaccessible steep hillsides, illustrating how important very rapid drainage is to success. Clearly cliff dwellers need very little surface water to survive. Overwatering and compacted soils are the chief reason why these plants fail in cultivation.

Echinocreus triglochidatus

Echinocreus engelmannii

Echinocereus engelmannii | **Hedgehog Cactus** | *Echinocereus triglochidatus* | **Claret Cup Cactus** | These two ground-hugging, clumping species are nearly identical to the untrained eye, but when they bloom you can clearly see the difference. *E. engelmannii* produces a larger 3-inch blossom in vivid magenta with striking yellow stamens. *E. triglochidatus* bears wine-red flowers that are smaller in size but numerous. In the wild it's not uncommon to find these cacti nestled against the south side of a large boulder or sprouting out of fissures in rocky cliffs where they access water trapped deep within the stone. These make excellent landscape plants provided they have not been illegally gathered from wildlands.

Opuntia basilaris | **Beaver Tail Cactus** | This ground-hugging, slow growing native lacks visible spines, but don't let that fool you. The small dots on its surface retain their painful glochids, and they are even present on the roots, so beware when handling and transplanting. What makes this a great landscape plant is its beautiful sky blue skin and abnormally large hot pink blossoms. Its habit spreads into low, wide patches that require very little water. In the wild plants will shrivel to twisted remnants only to quickly flesh out again after a rain. Use this wrinkling factor to tell you when it's in need of a drink. WARNING: The roots of this seemingly harmless cactus bear glochids too, so digging them out without protection can cause as much pain as contact with the stems.

Opuntia basilaris

Cylindropuntia bigelovii aka *Opuntia bigelovii* | **Teddy Bear Cholla** | Hardly docile, this teddy bear is the most ferocious in California. It shares a genus with the prickly pear, but differs in its cigar shaped upright stems. The segments are loosely connected so spines may grab onto passing wildlife and detach easily from the plant. This is how cholla self-propagates, because in general they do not produce much viable seed. The truly deadly spines are microscopically barbed and therefore hang on to their host tenaciously until it finally drops to the ground and immediately roots. Chollas are not advised in gardens with pets or children.

Opuntia basilaris

This juvenile paddle illustrates how leaves harden off to become spines and the "paddle" is actually the stem. Note the fine hair-like glochids at the base of each of the larger spines.

While this "teddy bear" variety lacks formidable thorns, it is more densely packed with glochids than any other *Opuntia*.

BEWARE OF OPUNTIA GLOCHIDS

Species of *Opuntia* which include all prickly pear and cholla cactus bear two types of spines within the round base known as a tubercle. The typically large, highly-visible spines are nestled into a tuft of near microscopic glochids. These glochids are hair-fine and so sharp they immediately penetrate the skin at the slightest touch. Just brush against them and they'll infest your clothing forever. Because the fibers are so delicate, glochids tend to break off at the surface of skin, clothing, gloves, or shoes, making them impossible to remove. Once inside a pocket you'll have to throw a jacket or shirt away. Prickly pear fruit is covered with glochids, making harvesting and skinning risky business. Because glochids infest gloves of all kinds, handle opuntias with barbecue tongs only. If you are accidentally attacked by glochids, do not try to brush them off. Try tweezers and a magnifying glass first. Then use masking tape to remove the remnants. Other methods of removing them are hair removal wax, glue, and bubble gum. Fresh aloe gel is recommended for treating the contact dermatitis that often follows a glochid infestation.

THREE FRUITING CACTI

The hotter the weather the sweeter the cactus fruit. The sweeter the fruit, the brighter its color. In the summer you'll see bright red fruit on cacti all over the valley. Growing your own fruiting cactus is also a great way to expand your culinary options. The key is to use those species which produce a plentiful supply of large fruit that's easy to harvest. The challenge is getting ripe fruit harvested before the birds consume it. Our avian friends seem to know the moment a red apple cactus reaches its peak of sweetness. As they near ripeness, some locals cover their ripening fruit with brown paper bags lightly tied around the stem to keep birds away.

Cereus peruvianus | **Peruvian Apple Cactus** | This branching columnar cactus is widely available, easy to grow, and produces the most delicious fruit. At maturity fruit is oval, 4 inches long, with orange-red skin that encloses snow white flesh studded with tiny black seeds. It's super sweet with seeds that crunch like sugar crystals. Harvest and immediately slice retaining rind to ensure they hold together. Arrange on a plate and refrigerate for a cold midsummer snack.

Opuntia ficus-indica | **Spineless Prickly Pear** | Thornless prickly pear produce large succulent fruit that ripens to deep red in the heat. It is a popular component of contemporary fresh Mexican cuisine. The juicy flesh is similar to that of honeydew melon and it is studded with BB-sized seeds. It is so plentiful the fruit is often crushed and strained to create sweet sauces, jams, and jellies. It's also skinned and eaten fresh. Plant a home orchard of Burbank's thornless variety which is far less painful to harvest. Keep in mind that hand peeling fruit can be risky. It's easier to grasp fruit with tongs and singe off glochids over the flame of a gas range or butane torch.

Cereus peruvianus

As fruit ripens on this cactus, protect from the birds using paper bags.

The snowy white flesh and crisp black seeds make the apple cactus the finest fruit for the kitchen.

Opuntia ficus-indica

Thornless prickly pear fruit still retains glochids which must be removed by burning or scraping to make handling pain-free.

Prickly pear fruit ranges in color from green to deep red depending on the variety and ripeness.

Hylocereus triangularis

Known as "dragon fruit" in the gourmet markets, the fruit of vine cactus looks and tastes similar to that of Peruvian apple cactus.

Hylocereus triangularis | **Queen of the Night** | Thick, three-sided vine cactus produces large round neon red fruit with flesh quite similar to that of the Peruvian apple cactus. This is a prolific bloomer that adapts to long fence lines and blooms much earlier from cutting-grown plants than the apple cactus. A fabulous looking, long blooming producer during the long summer months that can be used in a small garden or even trained up onto the roof or eaves where space is limited.

HOW TO BUY CACTI

Keep in mind that cacti are different than traditional plants because they store a great deal of moisture in the succulent tissues within their bodies. This means they aren't as dependent upon soil moisture. Their root systems can be small relative to the size of the plant. Therefore it's better to buy a big cactus in a small pot.

Cactophiles are big on bare root cacti which can remain out of the ground for quite some time before the plant's health is threatened. You are assured that a bare root specimen cactus retains a solid root system. Often cactus sold in larger pots will lose its root system to rot while on display, and you won't realize this until its time to transplant.

Cactus grown in containers, be they on your patio or in the grower's yard require, above all else, fast draining soil. When you water a cactus in a pot you are putting moisture in direct contact with the skin of the plant. It may sit there awhile before percolating down through the soil. If there's any irregularity in the cactus skin, be it a split, nick, or gouge, the water introduces pathogens into the tender internal succulent tissues of the cactus. Once contaminated, rot will slowly spread through the plant.

The only solution to a rotting cactus is to remove it from the soil altogether, then cut away the rotted portions until you reach healthy unaffected tissue. Allow this wound to dry and callus. Only then can you replant the cactus and hope no pockets of rot were left behind deeper in the plant's tissues.

In some cases cacti have been field grown. These cacti are dug up just before sale and potted to make them more appealing to retail garden center customers who don't know the value of bare root stock. Sometimes this temporary potting soil isn't ideal. It can be overwatered by novice staff while on display. Inspect your plants carefully at the garden center before you buy. Feel to see if the cactus is solidly anchored in the pot or loose to the touch. Loose cactus may have lost their roots to rot or were never properly rooted in the first place.

This illustrates how important it is to thoroughly inspect your cacti and strive for a blemish-free individual. Injuries aren't just dangerous to plant health, they can permanently disfigure a perfectly symmetrical cactus with ugly scar tissue. Likewise marks from burn or sunscald if sufficiently advanced last forever. Given the high cost of large cacti, you should insist on as perfect a plant as possible.

It can be tough to handle cacti in transport and at home, particularly if you're dealing with big specimens, glochid-rich opuntias, or vicious golden barrels. Be sure to wear gloves with thick leather on both the front and back of the hand. Work gloves with cloth backs offer no protection for your knuckles when reaching fingertips into the edge of a nursery pot to pick it up.

Some tips from Clark Moorten will help you handle these spiny fellows painlessly. "We use carpet padding to wrap up tall fence post cacti so we can move them without damaging their skin. When they're full of water they break easily because they're heavy. Carpet supports the entire length of the cactus equally. For larger plants like saguaro, short-nap dense carpet carries more weight and gives you something to grab when moving large ones to and from the truck." Moorten also advocates using spring-loaded long handled salad tongs. "We wrap the grabbing ends in duct tape so they're round because the sharp edges of the tongs will cut through the outer skin of most cacti."

The genus *Echinocereus* is often called rainbow cactus or collector's cactus because they produce such varied and exquisite flowers. This nearly thornless variety produces fabulous coral flowers in the spring, which are easily identified by the green stigmalobe at the center. Clark Moorten states that this became a catch-all genus for many cacti that defy further classification, which explains the diversity of size, spine density, and flower color of this immense group. Over time the use of DNA testing will no doubt reassign many to other genera.

CACTUS
SOIL MIX RECIPE

Plant only in commercially bagged soil designated for cacti and succulents to ensure proper drainage. If you need a greater quantity for large pots or raised planters, use Clark Moorten's recipe below. For larger or smaller quantities, adjust volumes accordingly.

- Two 5-gallon nursery pots of standard potting soil

- One 5-gallon nursery pot of coarse sand

- One 5-gallon nursery pot perlite

- 1/2- to 1-gallon nursery pot composed chicken manure

Cacti make perfect potted plants that offer bold architectural forms to small gardens, porches, and patios.

POTTING CACTI

The benefit of growing cacti in pots is that they're portable. Cacti can sit on a porch or patio all winter long to catch full sun, then moved to a more sheltered location during the summer. This eliminates the concern for sun damage, and you'll be able to rearrange your potted cacti with garden art and furniture to create fresh outdoor living areas each season.

Remember that you don't need overly large pots for cacti. Deep pots contain too much soil which can become extremely dry on top while the bottom is saturated. These wet bottoms introduce decomposing microorganisms into a cactus root system.

Cacti prefer wide open pans and bowls with large drain holes. This allows more surface area for water to percolate down into the root zone. Once you plant a wide pot, provide plenty of depth for a surface mulch of fine gravel. Gravel acts as an insulation layer keeping soil cooler and shaded in the summer. It also helps porous potting soil remain in place and reduces the chance of washout when you water to overflowing. Use a fine crushed gravel mulch that's free of accumulated dust.

RED CLAY | Cacti grow best in red clay because it breathes more like natural soil than stoneware or glazed pots. Mexican terra cotta is thicker, heavier, and darker in color than quality red clay. A year or two after planting in Mexican clay pots, the outer layers slough off to litter and stain your patio. The walls weaken too, and these can break apart under pressure of movement. If you want a fine home for quality cacti, insist on American or Italian terra cotta.

ABOVE: Small seedling cacti and other succulents can be purchased in cell packs, which are plastic trays of dozens of plugs, each containing one small plant. Cell packs are used by growers to pot up into 2-inch plastic pots, the smallest size you typically see at the nursery. Cell pack plants have a small wine-cork sized root ball that allows them to be planted very close together in pots and color bowls. This example shows how uniform cell pack seedlings grow, and a way they can be used to create geometric modern compositions in sleek contemporary containers. You may have to special order cell packs from succulent plant retailers.

RIGHT: This beautiful flower of *Echinopsis oxygona* is produced from a single small round potted cactus with a bloom stem over 6 inches long that extends out from the plant like an elephant's trunk. It blooms in the morning and is 5 inches across. It is an excellent example of how background color can make a blooming cactus stand out boldly in its setting whether outdoors or moved indoors to better enjoy the blossom. Species of genus *Echinopsis* are extensively bred to produce the largest, most outstanding flowers for small potted specimens ideally sized for porch or patio. Growing small cacti such as this in pots allows them to be grown in protected locations, then brought out into living areas temporarily to enjoy while in bloom.

The branching columnar *Myrtillocactus* is a perfect example of how a "crest" is one growing point that fans out to become many.

The serendipitous beauty of monstrose cacti make them popular among collectors.

FREAKS AND GEEKS IN THE CACTUS WORLD

Don't be afraid if your cactus suddenly changes into a monster. It's just an anomaly that sometimes shows up in succulents. Cacti are plants that produce a single growing point called the apical meristem. It is usually symmetrical in form, which is why the geometry of cactus plants is so picture perfect. But sometimes the growing point will multiply into many for no reason whatsoever. When this happens on one plane a cactus will develop a fan-shaped growth called a crest. It resembles a rooster's comb. Wild ferocactus on remote trails around the valley will sometimes produce crests. When the growing point multiplies in a more chaotic manner, growth occurs in many directions at once. The plant becomes strangely distorted into a monstrose form and yet grows healthy and large with time. These freaks of nature are rare and highly sought after as unique specimens for gardens.

EXOTIC CACTI FOR THE COACHELLA VALLEY

The world of cacti is complicated by the fact that most cactus species look alike to the untrained eye. Even cactophiles have a hard time keeping up with frequent changes in the botanical names. As a Coachella Valley gardener, the best approach is to go on a "need to know" basis with your cacti. If you don't need to know the name, don't worry about it! Rather than try to be all-inclusive, this section features some of the more common types of cacti found in our local landscapes. All of them will be a good bet for your garden provided they are in the right place for their preferred exposure.

Echinocactus grusonii | **Golden Barrel Cactus** | Fabulous golden yellow spines are held so densely they obscure the flowers and make the whole plant glow when backlit. This barrel originates in Mexico and is now almost extinct in the wild. It is the favorite cactus for creating geometrically spaced masses of cacti in modern style landscapes. They fit well into naturalistic compositions as well as traditional pots and bowls. Golden barrels thrown out in our valley sun languish and eventually die. If well positioned and watered generously in the summer, they grow very quickly. Provide a southern exposure and some protection in the depths of summer.

Echinocactus grusonii

Myrtillocactus geometrizans | **Myrtle Cactus** | This fast growing branching tree-like green cactus is truly vigorous. It is used as rootstocks for grafted cactus proving just how reliable it can be. The blue-green branches are edged with widely spaced stubby spines. Blossoms are small followed by red berry-like fruit. While this modest blooming sets it apart from more colorful cacti, the resilient nature of this species makes it a good architectural form.

Pachycereus marginatus | **Fence Post Cactus** | This tall ribbed cactus is among the easiest of the larger forms to cultivate. It's also widely available, and its fast growth means it's less expensive to buy. Often planted as living fences in their homeland of Mexico, they are quite resilient here in the desert. It produces many new branches from the base to a height of 18 feet, but just 4 feet wide.

Pachycereus marginatus

Myrtillocactus geometrizans

The most sensitive species of cacti from Madagascar are grown in the controlled environment of the world's first cactarium at Moorten Botanical Garden.

The age of Moorten Botanical Garden provides a wealth of mature specimens raised in the local desert climate.

This historic old house at the center of the garden was built in the 1920s.

LOCATION: MOORTEN BOTANICAL GARDEN

Nestled behind mesquite trees along South Palm Canyon lies an extraordinary garden of cacti and desert plants. Created over sixty years ago by Chester "Cactus Slim" Moorten and his wife, Patricia, this acre and a half has reached maturity. Many of the specimens have achieved monolithic proportions and are truly a unique site in a valley only recently populated. Within the confines of their family home is a densely planted landscape of desert dwellers collected over many decades. Today it is managed by Clark Moorten, their only child, born to the cactus trade.

Within Moorten Botanical Garden the plants are grouped by region of origin. The collection of tall South American cacti is truly stunning due to its diversity. Because the Moortens made many trips into Baja California and Mexico during Clark's youth, their collection is strong in natives of that region. A single rare bursera tree is believed to be the largest in California. Arranged in a beautiful setting combined with a vast collection of fossils, minerals, petrified wood, and old west relics, this garden is a rare vestige of an earlier time. It remains vitally important for its collections. Stroll the paths which will prove exactly what grows in the Coachella Valley, what kind of exposure is needed, and how young plants will eventually behave at maturity.

Moorten Botanical Garden
1701 South Palm Canyon Drive
Palm Springs, CA 92264 (760) 327-6555

THIS CHAPTER IN A NUTSHELL

(1) Very few cacti grow out on the valley floor. They are far more prevalent on the sloping foothills where they are protected from the sun and wind and are assured good drainage.

(2) *Opuntia* species which include prickly pear and cholla, bear microscopic glochids which are hair-like spines that cause serious contact dermatitis.

(3) Cacti can have much smaller root systems than you might expect, and need little soil to grow large and healthy, provided they are well drained.

(4) Save money by buying large specimen cacti as bare root plants rather than in containers.

(5) Use salad or barbecue tongs to handle cactus plants. Try carpet and carpet padding to wrap larger species for pain- and damage-free transport.

CHAPTER 5

LOW DESERT STAPLES

The low desert staple is a plant that grows so well here it's a no-brainer. Many are in bloom in nearly every season. They're unlikely to suffer sunburn or frost damage. Look for proof of their success in roadway medians and parking lots where they thrive despite intense reflected heat from seas of pavement. These plants are the cast iron species fundamental to our desert landscape.

For year-round residents, summer color is a valuable commodity. In fact, some of these rugged species take on their best color in excessive heat. Snowbirds rarely see the Mexican bird of paradise in its summer glory because it waits for temperatures to be consistently over the century mark to bloom.

The flip side to these species' nature is their tendency to outgrow the space provided in a short year or two after planting. Because the desert climate supports plant life year-round, there's no dormant season to check their growth. Professional gardeners make a living hacking back this rampant growth on a monthly, and sometimes even weekly basis. Nearly all these plants are important hummingbird nectar sources. They are equally as appealing to butterflies of all stripes. Other forms of wildlife from big black mason bees to finches and moths all find these plants to be valuable food sources in the often sparse desert summer.

Since these are the core material of your landscape, the profile of each plant or plant group will be more extensive than anywhere else in this book. Pay attention to the details of size and color options because some offer a huge array of choices.

THE BOUGAINVILLEA

No flower defines old Palm Springs like the bougainvillea. Masses of intense color draped the Spanish style buildings of the early village. They cloaked gateways and climbed into trees to provide the only bright spots in the dead heat of summer. It is the stress of heat and drought that makes them bloom so abundantly.

This South American vine is technically a liana, which are tropical vines that grow into the canopy of equatorial forests. They've been bred into a vast array of colors from snow-white to deep red, orange, gold, and purple. What many think are

its flowers are in fact bracts—uniquely colored leaves. They are designed to lure pollinators to the very tiny tubular flowers sequestered inside the huge clusters of bracts.

They tend to produce flushes of "blooms" which then fall and are quickly replaced by new ones. Some individuals will shed bracts all year-round, which produces a perpetual litter problem. Paper light bracts are easily blown into swimming pools, fill car ports, and clog flower beds. The typical solution is to shear them into tightly branched hedge-like masses which limits both color and natural rangy beauty.

Bougies produce a huge mass of very fine roots that are sensitive to disturbance. It's next to impossible to transplant an existing bougie at all. Growers propagate them in a very sandy soil mix that lacks cohesiveness for absolute drainage. If the root ball disintegrates while transplanting, you may lose the plant altogether. When planting a large one, it's best to dig the hole, set the potted bougie in the bottom, then cut away the pot in pieces to ensure the root ball remains intact.

Most bougies are sold exclusively by bract color. These are most often the very large liana forms that can exceed 30 feet in height and width over time. A single San Diego Red can engulf a small house! Fortunately, breeding has produced smaller varieties to keep you from becoming overwhelmed. Shorter forms including the Australian Bambino series were developed to behave more like shrubs than vines. They make fine groundcover or can be used as a freestanding shrub. Insist on labels at the garden center to ensure you've got the dwarf and not a big one pruned short to look like a dwarf. They're all identical as juveniles.

Very pale blush shades of bougainvillea are beautiful, but won't retain their color in the desert sun. Many bleach to white in direct exposure, and if they're grown in shade they refuse to bloom at all. Choose bold colors whenever possible.

EXCEPTIONAL BOUGIES

While all bougies do well in the desert, here are a few unique varieties that offer specific benefits or unusual forms.

Purple Queen | Just take a look at the dark green leaves of this bougie and you'll see it's different from the rest. Aside from its unique look, its other benefit is the fact that the bracts don't detach from the plant right away. They remain on the plant for weeks, even months, fading gradually over time. When they fade too much, pluck them off the vine by hand. You won't have the litter with Purple Queen, and you can plant it without concern for excessive maintenance. This is an intermediate-sized plant that grows up to 15 feet long.

Bambino Bougies | From an Australian breeder come the Bambino series of dwarf bougainvilleas. They not only offer a full range of colors, many of them feature variegated foliage too. The Bambinos average about 3 feet tall and wide, growing in a dense mound. They are distinguished by their "baby" names such 'Baby Alyssa' (white), 'Baby Lauren' (lavender), and 'Baby Victoria' (magenta). While other "dwarf" forms of bougainvillea are available, it's important to check with your local garden center before you buy. Some of these are merely smaller in stature than the big 30-footers, but are still too large to be considered shrub or groundcover.

Torch Glow | This is a unique variety developed from a tree-like South American species. Its upright form stands like a shrub and requires no support. Red-pink bracts stand atop upward angled branches. They are slower growing, up to 6 feet tall, and 3 feet wide.

ABOVE RIGHT: Purple Queen

BELOW RIGHT: Torch Glow

Salvia greggii | **Autumn Sage** | hybrids | 3' tall, 3' wide | Hummingbirds are irresistibly lured to these plants, with heavy bloomers jealously guarded by dominant males. This is actually a sub-shrub, which grows quickly to bloom like a perennial, but its structure is woody. The original red flowered species, *Salvia greggii* is native to New Mexico, Texas, and northern Mexico where it prefers dry washes. When breeders began working with these plants, the standard red exploded into a wide range of pinks and white. The purple seems to be afflicted with lesser vigor and may not perform well here. The newer bicolored flowers are equally unproven. Feel free to shop for these plants by flower color because they are always in bloom at the garden center.

What makes autumn sage hybrids so useful is their open, airy character that makes them semitransparent. This lends a charming cottage garden look that blends well with more traditional-looking desert perennials such as the penstemons. Sage blooms modestly year-round in full sun, but is most prolific in the dead heat of summer.

Keep in mind that brittle branching and weak joints make this sage vulnerable to breakage. It's best to locate your autumn sage away from walkway areas and pools where cleaning equipment or a garden hose can easily damage a plant. To encourage stronger branching, trim them vigorously while young to produce a more dense habit. Don't be surprised if they lose vigor after a few years. Don't hesitate to replace them as required.

TOP: *Salvia greggii* pink hybrid
BOTTOM: *Salvia greggii* red

Tecoma stans | **Yellow Bells** | This is one of the most under appreciated shrubs in the desert. Few large shrubs bloom so heavily with large flowers valuable to wildlife. It's native from the American Southwest into Mexico where it goes by the name *esperanza*. These shrubs thrive despite poor soils, heat, and scant rainfall proving they are exceptional choices for desert gardens.

Tecoma is exceptionally fast growing and reaches 12 feet tall by 6 feet wide in just a few years. Its upright habit produces long flexible branches topped with huge clusters of tubular flowers. The 5-inch trumpets hardly look like rugged desert natives, yet they flower continuously in all but the darkest winter months. As natives they are so well adapted that seed shed will readily self-sow in sandy soils. These will revert to the standard yellow species and easily transplant to other parts of your garden.

Breeding has produced some named cultivars with improved flowers. 'Gold Star' blooms more often and in larger clusters than the native.

Don't overlook the orange flowered hybrids which are nothing short of spectacular. They have proven themselves time and again to equal the species in extremes of heat and frost. Vigorous and upright growing, they make exceptional background shrubs. The flowers are smaller than the yellow, but clusters produce far more individuals. Some bloom so heavily they cause the branches to arch under the weight. Large black bees find these absolutely irresistible with the blossoms literally dripping with nectar. Beware of where you plant them to avoid bee conflicts and possible spotting of pavement. Look for varieties 'Burnt Out,' 'Orange Jubilee,' and 'Sunrise,' all of which are perfect candidates for a specimen, privacy screens, informal hedges, and as lush background.

RIGHT: *Tecoma stans* 'Orange Jubilee'

Tecomaria capense | **Cape Honeysuckle** | This South African shrub is perfectly adapted to the long dry season and extreme heat of its homeland, which makes it perfect for desert gardens. Named for its large flowers that resemble those of honeysuckle, it is another hummingbird favorite.

Cape honeysuckle is a chameleon. Chop it back into a tightly branched shrub or a long hedge. Train on the vertical for a wall of privacy-giving foliage. Allow it to drape over ugly fences to disguise them with a lush green background. But above all, don't shear it or you'll sacrifice the blossoms.

Flowers are intense orange, but there is a less common yellow flowered 'Aurea' variety. Both bloom heavily in the heat extending well into the winter and often year-round. Unlike many other shrubs used for hedging, this beauty is solidly frost resistant so there's no worry of losing privacy from frost burn.

Cape honeysuckle tends to develop long flexible runner-like growth which can become gangly if not adequately shaped. It'll travel along the ground if allowed to flop, rooting as it grows. This is helpful if you're trying to create a screen because you won't have to plant so many originals to get coverage. The whips can be guided back up into the parent plant or allowed to root where they lie. Once rooted you can detach from the mother to create a whole new plant somewhere else.

Thevetia peruviana | **Chinese Oleander** | Though it's related to the common oleander, this South American species is thankfully disease free. Lush rich green foliage is a beautiful background for the large yellow trumpet flowers produced in the heat of summer. Fast growing and widely adaptable, this plant can, with pruning, take on a variety of forms.

It's technically a shrub suitable to replace the oleander. In old neighborhoods of Palm Springs there are hedges of them sheared to a tight wall of leaves that fail to bloom as prodigiously as the naturally shaped plants. Although references state these shrubs grow up to 8 feet tall, in our valley they will easily exceed this to reach tree-sized proportions if not battered by wind.

This makes a fine small tree for tight spaces. If pruned well in the early years they'll branch more densely. Beware of the white sap exuded during pruning because it is as toxic as that of the common oleander and the foliage will be equally as poisonous to children and pets. Plants grow best on an east facing exposure in full morning sun, but they are able to thrive in a more open exposure as well.

? WHAT HAPPENED TO ALL THE OLEANDERS?

For decades the oleander was the most important plant in southern California. It was all things to all people, providing important landscaping solutions with beautiful color. In Palm Springs they were planted as hedgerows for reducing wind, increasing privacy, and to catch drifting sand. These cast iron beauties were the quintessential desert staple until the early 1990s.

Enter oleander leaf scorch (OLS), caused by the bacterium, *Xylella fastidiosa*, which is highly infectious. It clogs the xylem tubes that carry water from the roots to foliage. This explains why the foliage of an infected plant grows smaller as it gradually succumbs. Eventually there isn't enough water to support the foliage and the plant dies back to the ground, leaving a skeleton of dry sticks. Sadly there is no cure and it is possible that most, if not all oleanders in the Coachella Valley will eventually be affected. Ficus and Carolina cherry have gradually replaced the oleander hedges.

Caesalpinia pulcherrima | **Mexican Bird of Paradise** | Without question, this is the undisputed queen of the summer. It's an open, wispy shrub with fern-like foliage that's lovely in its own right. But when days are blistering hot this beauty blooms up a summer storm. Atop long wand-like stems sit the most incredibly vivid blossoms of red-orange with yellow highlights. They bloom for months on end providing beautiful focal points for windows of an air conditioned home.

This shrub does best in open, dry landscapes with a lot of space. It is impervious to reflected pavement heat and some of the best specimens in town are planted along curbs, sidewalks and in parking lots. It's a fast grower—up to about 10 feet tall and wide. The down side is that no matter what you do the plants look crummy in the winter when they become partially or completely deciduous. This is when the gardeners cut them back to reduce visibility. But fast growth and speedy bloom on the new growth will bring them back to their former selves come summer.

THE LANTANAS

Nothing fills space with color as quickly and thoroughly as lantana. It's one of the few plants capable of naturalizing here and self sows so effectively it can easily become a problem. Today's lantanas are complex hybrids with flowers that take on multiple colors as a single cluster ages. This color variation is due to the fact that they are always in a process of creating new florets at the center while dropping old ones around the edges. A floret that opens yellow will age to orange and finally to red as it reaches the outer edge of the cluster. Named varieties feature different color progressions, which is what makes these plants so versatile.

The fragrance of lantana foliage is unmistakably pungent. The twig surfaces are slightly barbed, making them uncomfortable to handle without gloves. Flowers are followed by berries eaten by birds, which increase the potential for volunteers to pop up unexpectedly. Some of the bigger lantanas grow so quickly they are downright weedy and may overwhelm smaller yards.

To enjoy this plant which can color a yard in a matter of weeks, you need to know how lantana varieties differ. They can be divided into three groups related to growth habit and size. This will also help you select the right one for the application you have in mind.

Lantana montevidensis

Lantana montevidensis | **Trailing Lantana** | This single species is available in just one color: purple, although a purple and white mix is known. Its leaves are small, grey-green in color, the growth habit ground-hugging. They grow remarkably fast in the heat making a super quick to mature groundcover for new homesites that need some relief from bare ground. This plant is often found on highway medians because it won't grow so tall that it obscures traffic. Growth is dense enough to effectively block weeds. Runners may root as they spread.

Because this is the only cool colored lantana, it's popular to mix with spreading and bush lantanas that feature hot hued blooms. When they grow together into a single mass, the effect is truly eye popping. Blend with bright yellow spreading lantana for a feast of complementary colors.

Lantana hot pink

Spreading lantana

Spreading Lantana | These are hybrids of the very low and very wide ranging lantanas. They were bred for growing in containers and for use in smaller city sized gardens. Most are used for groundcover with a wider range of color. The foliage is more like the larger bush lantanas, dark green and lush. They'll grow just 2 to 3 feet tall and spread to about 4 feet or more in diameter. A superior filler for narrow beds or along the edge of concrete. Colors are many shades of yellow and orange-red. Grow this lantana in big pots around the swimming pool for beautiful color without litter or concern for reflected heat.

Lantana camara | **Bush Lantana** | Big bush lantana offers the most spectacular flower colors of all. Their wide range of colors in a single cluster makes them extremely popular, particularly because of their ability to bloom prolifically all year-round. In fact, the hotter and drier they are, the more heavily they bloom. This illustrates how a bit of neglect can result in more incredible color.

The most common color combination is the red-orange-yellow range, but don't settle for these if you want a different look in mind. There is a luscious yellow to soft flamingo pink that's very cottage gardenesque. Another that features golden yellow to neon hot pink is a delightful bright spot in tropical and modern gardens. A dozen variations on these offer a huge range of choices, so shop blooming plants by eye appeal.

Bush lantana can grow to mega proportions in Palm Springs because there's little frost to knock it back. Because plants grow vigorously in the summer, the best time to cut them back is in the late fall to make room for annual filler plants. Allowing lantanas to spread and cover in the summer shades the soil and keeps it cooler for the other trees and shrubs around them.

Lantana camara

Leucophyllum frutescens | **Texas Ranger** | A native of the Southwest, this shrub produces beautiful grey foliage that protects it from the sun. The color makes an exceptional plant for Mediterranean-style homes because it's foliage and flowers evokes that of lavender, a signature of that region's landscape. But lavender struggles in the desert while Texas ranger thrives! If occasionally clipped while young, its normal rangy form can become quite tame, producing a great bloomer that perfectly accents stacked stone and stucco facades.

This clan has also benefited from recent breeding with other *Leucophyllum* species to expand the range of flower color and plant size. There are darker purple, blue, and white flowered forms as well as some with greener foliage. Taller varieties make exceptional hedges that may be sheared, but this will sacrifice its great color display. Like other desert staples, Texas rangers grow all over town in parking lots where it's often the only plant that survives battering and neglect.

Leucophyllum frutescens

Pennisetum setaceum

THE GRASSES

Ornamental grasses are a relative newcomer to Palm Springs, but since they arrived the desert landscape has never been the same. They've proven to be incredibly successful here in the desert, offering a whole new look to our desert gardens. They are soft and sexy, growing animated in the slightest breeze. They're adapted to mass planting, creating truly dramatic effects in Spartan surroundings.

Exceptional stands can be seen in front of the newly reconstructed Biltmore Hotel on East Palm Canyon and in the median approach to El Paseo in Palm Desert. Virtually no naturalistic composition is without them. Each year new species are appearing to expand the color and size options for desert gardeners. Not all of these will be successful, but some may be so well adapted they'll escape to become weeds.

The beauty of the grasses is augmented by their flowers held high above the foliage for wind pollination. They spike in late summer and fall, holding their bloom heads through the winter. Mature flowers in the fall season make these plants a star performer for the start of our local social season.

Grasses that have evolved in cooler climates die back into dormancy as the days grow short. Those that originate in Africa and other equatorial climates offer a better year-round specimen. But even these will require occasional renewal by hard pruning because in their original habitats, bush fires and wildlife would renew them much the same way. Without renewal they produce excess chaff which gets in the way of new luxurious growth and bloom spikes.

Pennisetum setaceum | **Fountain Grass** | This was the first grass to bless desert landscapes. Its fountain-like form when in bloom explains the name. It's a big burly fellow and one of the most beautiful of all grasses. The species includes many cultivars, but it's the 'Rubrum' variety that is the most common. It is valued for its purple tinted foliage and multicolored flower heads that range from cream to lavender and maroon all on the same plant. This is a tropical grass that thrives in the heat but may prove slow growing during the winter months.

Festuca glauca | **Blue Fescue** | Long before the current ornamental grass craze, the mid-century modern crowd was fawning over blue fescue in the '60s. This tightly knit dome of clear blue fine needle foliage features a uniformity of growth that like barrel cactus, can be used in geometric arrangements to create visual interest in spare modern gardens. It's equally perfect for spotting into dry stream beds or to use around rock outcroppings. Blue fescue is particularly wonderful in streamlined modern-looking pots. But when blue fescue blooms with little blond spikes of feathery flowers, it takes on a much more casual look, and the overall color changes to a more pale hue. Modern gardeners may choose to snip the spikes off as soon as they appear and to gently shape the dome-like form for a more precise profile.

Festuca glauca

Nassella tenuissima | **Mexican Feather Grass** | Few grasses can compete with the fine texture of this feather grass. It's a beautiful arching shorter grass with blades thin as horse hair produced in dense clumps. Exceptional for smaller gardens, it contrasts incredibly with succulents and other desert plants. Blooms are about as long as the foliage, feathery and beige colored. As clumps mature the inner core of the grass may die out resulting in an empty center. In early winter dig the clumps up and separate them into smaller pieces to replant. Another option is to let this grass go to seed and let the seedlings pop up in next year's landscape for an ever-changing layout.

OTHER GRASSES
FOR DESERT GARDENS

For each of the species below are many cultivars that vary in size and color.

Cortaderia selloana	Pampas Grass
Muhlenbergia capillaries	Pink Muhly
Muhlenbergia rigens	Deer Grass
Panicum virgatum	Switch Grass

Nassella tenuissima

Whitewater Rock and Supply is located at the Whitewater Exit from I-10 just west of Palm Springs.

LOCATION: WHITEWATER ROCK AND SUPPLY CO.

Sitting beside Highway 10 at the Whitewater exit, just west of Palm Springs sprawls a 25-acre world-class rock yard. The rock yard grew out of Al Bankus' mine that can be seen on the hillside just east of the site from the west valley. There he discovered a unique quartsite which bears a warm gold color with naturally occurring feldspar that gives it a unique glittering quality. Dubbed "Palm Springs Gold," it is exclusive to Whitewater and sold in many forms, from large chunks to fine sand-like surfacing material. When laid out on exposed soil and watered, fine Palm Springs Gold packs down to create a hard crust that reduces erosion and weeds. This material has been used since the '60s around the valley. Al's son, Allan Bankus, owns and manages the operation today which includes a fleet of trucks for hauling and special equipment for setting boulders on any site. A stroll through this museum of stone reveals the greatest assortment of materials in the state. They specialize in slabs of sandstone, quartzite and slate for steppers, paving and outdoor table tops in various natural colors. Dozens of colors of crushed and river-run gravel offer a huge range of surfacing materials. On any day you'll find over 2,000 types of stone from around the world. There are even authentic adobe bricks, granite monoliths, and chunks of petrified wood. Whitewater sells to both contractors and the public. On-site scales help you weigh your vehicle, fill it, then weigh again to make your purchase by the pound or ton. Gardeners and visitors are welcome to stroll through this remarkable site and become thoroughly inspired. Closed Sundays.

Create fabulous desert rock gardens with gourmet stone sold as individual pieces, in palettes, or by the truckload.

Whitewater Rock carries the valley's most extensive selection of stone in slab, chunk, and hewn units.

Whitewater Rock and Supply Co.

58645 Old Highway 60

Whitewater, CA 92282

(760) 325-2747

www.whitewater-rock.com

THIS CHAPTER IN A NUTSHELL

(1) One of the best new additions to desert gardens is the dwarf "Bambino" series of bougainvillea from Australia.

(2) Native shrub, *Tecoma stans* and its varieties are little known but should be far more widely grown in the valley for its big color, water conservation, and wildlife value.

(3) Oleanders are being decimated by disease and should not be replanted as there is no cure. Try Cape Honeysuckle, Chinese Oleander and Hedge Fig as alternatives.

(4) Small container-grown nursery lantanas can be trailing, spreading, or bush forms in a spectacular array of colors; read the label carefully to select the right growth habit of the floral hues you love.

(5) Do not plant ornamental grasses upwind from a swimming pool.

CHAPTER 6

THE DESERT COTTAGE GARDEN

The love of floral cottage gardens is universal, and fortunately they can be part of our desert landscape if you know what plants lend this unique character. A cottage garden is quite simply a collection of perennials and some flowering shrubs arranged in a casual way. This is because such gardens evolved in the yards of everyday flower lovers, and they aren't bound by many of the rules of design that govern more highbrow layouts.

It's the color and the way you arrange your perennials that gives this landscape such charm. Planting designers are well aware that it's the form and color of a perennial that is most powerful, not its place of origin. Using desert-hardy plants that bear spikes, masses, or bushes of color can together recreate the look and feel of more traditional flower gardens from cooler climates. This is a far better solution than trying to force the northern plants to grow here.

Perennials bloom year after year without replanting, ensuring you enjoy more color as they mature into ever larger clumps. Some may even self-sow if conditions are right. Most can be divided with time into even more plants. Sure, you can augment them with seasonal annuals, but with perennials you won't be tied to that costly and laborious task of replanting masses every October.

The western states and regions extending well into Mexico are populated with an extraordinary array of native perennials. Hummingbirds and butterflies recognize the flowers and flock to them for abundant nectar. Other perennials which hail from desert regions around the world may also find a place in this garden.

The chief reason gardeners have chosen difficult northern species over desert-adapted perennials is simply because they don't recognize the natives. In the past the natives weren't available to buy because few wholesalers grew them. Today the demand for desert-adapted perennials has made them available to garden centers such as Moller's and The Living Desert, which carry them in small sizes at a very reasonable price.

Beware of purchasing perennials from larger national chain stores. Buyers often live far from your local store and have no conception of desert extremes. You'll see an incredible range of perennials in stock, but few of them will be long-lived here. In fact, many won't last more than a single season. Even the exotic kangaroo paw from Australia may not be sustainable here and are best treated as annuals. Your ability to recognize the desert plants amidst larger displays will guide your hand in choosing good species that will perform beautifully year after year.

WHAT MAKES A COTTAGE GARDEN?

A cottage garden is quite simply a casual flower garden. It is typically composed of perennials that are long-lived and bloom every year. The plants are easy to grow, floriferous choices that produce an abundance of color in a wide range of forms. The way you arrange the shapes and color influences how the garden will look.

In other chapters of this book, plants are predominately vivid, hot-colored flowers. Reds, oranges, and yellow are most prevalent among heat-loving species. But cottage garden lovers are often enchanted by the softer tones of cool hues that seem to thwart the heat of the day. The preference for lavender, pink, purple, blue white, and pale lemon yellow are strong contenders for this palette. An occasional red or orange adds depth and interest, but only when used in moderation.

However, cottage gardens can be bright and bold, so don't hesitate to draw plants from "Desert Staples" in chapter 5—particularly the salvias and bougainvilleas. It's purely driven by personal preference—the hues you love, those that work with your décor, and blend with the ambiance of your outdoor living spaces.

MANIPULATING COLOR | Creating flower gardens that really appeal to the eye is an art, and thus will follow color theory of the painter. In gardens we work with analogous colors and complementary colors. The ability to manipulate these concepts by plant grouping will have a big impact on how satisfying the cottage garden is for you.

On the color wheel you will find analogous colors adjacent to one another. They blend gently with little abrupt change in hue. A cool-tone garden as described above is a perfect example with blues, purples, and grays.

The complementary colors are opposite one another on the wheel. These create the most profound contrast when placed side by side in the garden. Examples are blue and yellow or red and green. The contrast can be so great that the human eye sees an actual vibration where they intersect. This creates a far more exciting dynamic for gardens created as festive places for fun and entertaining.

The combination of light and dark when blending complementary colors creates bold visual character.

MANIPULATING HEIGHT | What makes cottage gardens so great is diversity. Big flowers and tiny ones, tall spikes and ground-hugging mats come together here. You'll lose this great character if you stick with similar heights and forms. Then it simply becomes an ordinary mass planting. In true cottage style, strive for as much variation in height and texture as possible while sticking with your desired color palette.

In the garden, every plant deserves to be seen, and every plant needs an equal amount of light. These two factors govern how we arrange plants according to their height and form to prevent taller species from shading out shorter ones behind them. Therefore you plant the tallest bloomers to the rear of the garden, with the plants of intermediate height in front of them. In the very foreground of the garden go the ground-hugging plants. In an island planter with plenty of light on all sides, the tallest plants stand at the center with breaks to allow light to pass between them; then you work your heights out toward the edge.

French and Spanish lavenders can add a fragrant blue and grey combination, but only in the right location.

GROUPS | Cottage gardens disappoint when too sparsely planted. It is the density and the riot of color that makes them so appealing. But many desert perennials can be rather spindly if planted as a single specimen. The best way to compound their density of color and long range visibility in larger gardens is to plant in groups of three or more. This intensifies their presence and makes the color contrasts really pop.

PLANTING | Due to the narrow window of planting in the desert, typically around the month of October, plants have only a short time to acclimate to their new location before the brief, cold snap of winter. If planted from very small seedlings, both annuals and perennials have a difficult time becoming established. Although it is more costly, planting from larger more mature container grown plants is advisable to ensure a great

show the first year. It also helps plants root deep into native soil, where it is cool enough to withstand the coming summer.

Although some perennials are sold in six packs, it is advisable to avoid them in favor of quart sizes. One gallon is the ideal size because these are strong, well-established plants that can bloom well immediately. This is particularly true with native plants that may be more sensitive to root disturbance and transplanting than garden varieties.

ANNUAL STRATEGIES FOR PERENNIAL GARDENS

What really sets the Coachella Valley golf courses and communities apart from the rest of the desert southwest is our long standing tradition of annual bedding flower displays. Planted in October, these densely planted masses of color pop out of island planters through fall and winter until the end of the social season, with some blooming deep into the summer months. It's typical to change out entire beds each year, which requires a whole new design and color palette to be created from scratch.

For cottage gardeners, you must work around the structure of your permanent perennials with these seasonal additions. Most perennials don't bloom until March, so your annuals must carry the garden for color in the meantime. In the first years of a brand new perennial garden, the plants will appear sparse and unappealing. Using seasonal color to compensate until things mature is a great way to avoid that unattractive adolescent stage.

Annuals should not overwhelm the space and compete with the beauty of your more long-lived plants, so a light hand is best. Think like a watercolor artist rather than with potent van Gogh hues. Give each plant plenty of space to grow and bloom instead of packing them in carpet-like as they do with display bedding.

Since desert perennials tend to be spread out, annuals with short stature and a spreading form such as verbena are some of the best fillers for these gardens. The trailing Wave petunias are considered among the

Hanging baskets of annuals such as these dwarf petunia provide long-lasting cottage garden color without disturbing the in-ground garden.

most vigorous choices, far more reliable than other petunia forms. You'll notice there are not many French marigolds in desert gardens because they simply don't perform well here. But their larger African marigold cousins are much happier in our climate.

One of the most difficult colors to obtain in desert plants is blue. Annuals are a great way to bring many shades of it into the garden to cool out an over-abundance of hot-colored bougainvilleas and oleanders. Explore the viola clan which offers a staggering array of light to dark blue varieties. Their smaller flowers will not flop over under sprinkler water weight as the pansies do.

The character of the container you choose has a lot to do with the way a plant fits into the garden. Although this container is planted with succulents, they take on the look of an English cottage garden simply by how soft pastel hues blend with the pale terra cotta pedestal urn.

Blue-flowered *Salvia farinacea* is a strong and long-lived source of blue.

Gallardia

HIGH-IMPACT SEASONAL COLOR

Some plants treated as annuals here can be perennial or biennial in other climates. They're usually sold in quarts or 1-gallon pots, nearly mature and in full bloom. Using these to give you instant color for a party or special event, or to compensate for a newly planted landscape is the best way to punch up visual quality overnight. But don't expect them to last forever. Some will wither around the summer solstice and may cease to bloom or die altogether, unable to take the soaring and often sudden heat.

The success of Iceland poppy here in the desert as an annual cannot be overstated. It's delicate beauty and high visual profile lends a European look when grown with the salvias and penstemons.

Margeurites are a large family of daisy-bearing bushes bred into a range of colors. These include the Euryops clan with their bright yellow blossoms. These big bushes sold in one and two gallon containers produce delightful mounds that are much like the asters of northern climates but bloom during winter and spring. They can be trimmed gently from time to time to produce a new flush of blooms. Plant these to fill gaps in the cottage garden with reliable, long-term color.

LOCALLY NATIVE WILDFLOWERS TO SOW INTO COTTAGE GARDENS

Lupinus arizonicus	Arizona lupine
Eschscholzia californica	California poppy
Rafinesquia neomexicana	Desert chicory
Malacothrix glabrata	Desert dandelion
Eschscholzia parishii	Desert poppy
Abronia villosa	Sand verbena
Phacelia distans	Wild heliotrope

California poppy

The locally native *Lupinus arizonicus* prefer sunny, well-drained sites.

Yellow encelia and purple desert verbena are complementary colors that create a bold high-contrast combination.

The desert dandelion, *Malacothrix glabrata* creates a solid carpet of lemon yellow.

MO TIPS

Sow seed of desert wildflowers in the fall. You'll find locally adapted mixtures with California poppy and desert verbena at the Living Desert and Moller's Garden Center. They make outstanding displays in early spring if there are plentiful rains, or if provided with water periodically during dry winters. They are a great way to add color to neglected corners, and some truly spectacular stands can be seen around the valley for weeks in spring. Oddly enough, residents sow them into their crushed gravel surfaces because wildflowers don't require much coverage to sprout and bloom. That's why they pop up in the most unexpected places.

The Coachella Valley's own species of California poppy features a larger plant with smaller flowers and more of them. Bright yellow *Eschscholzia munutiflora* is best hand sown from seed into well-drained sandy or gravelly soil. This specimen prefers to tap moisture trapped beneath the adjacent boulders in Chino Canyon.

In the early morning you'll find *Datura discolor* blooming all over the valley. This very toxic nightshade played an important role in Native American coming-of-age ceremonies. It is highly attractive to the hummingbird moths which can be seen fluttering about them at dawn. It is a large sprawling perennial of gray-green leaves that makes a fabulous addition to the night garden, reflecting moonlight from its huge, snow-white trumpet flowers. Collect seed from the prickly "thornapple" pods to plant in gardens where there is no risk of poisoning to pets or children.

The delicate ground-hugging desert star, *Monoptilon bellioides* is a wonderful example of the tiny wildflowers that cover the desert floor in the early spring. Often included in desert wildflower seed mixes, it is among the many dainty beauties too often overlooked in favor of the more visible brittlebush and desert verbena.

PLANTS FOR THE PERENNIAL DESERT GARDEN

The plants that follow are the core palette for the desert cottage garden. They offer intense hot color and muted floral options for multihue compositions. There are spike flowers and blooming domes of foliage, but all feature an extended season of color with minimal water and care. In keeping with the design of perennial borders, we've grouped these plants according to height.

LOW GROWERS

Cuphea llavea | **Bat-Faced Cuphea** | 2' tall, 3' wide | Named for the big-eared bat-like faces of its inch-wide flowers, this gregarious heat loving perennial deserves far more attention. Intensely colored red "ears" over a deep purple "face" make them truly stunning. Blooming continuously throughout the hot months until midwinter cold, they are truly carefree perennials. This is a frost tender annual native to Michoacan, Mexico that may become perennial if protected from early morning cold. In sandy desert soils its volunteers pop up on their own, but coloring in these may vary to less intense shades of pink and lavender. Seedlings readily transplant. Plants prefer sheltered locations with even moisture such as courtyards or beneath tree canopies where they are protected from direct afternoon sun.

Epilobum cana | **California Fuchsia** | 1–2' tall, 4' wide | This vivid lipstick-orange flowering perennial is also known as hummingbird trumpet because it lures the little birds like crazy. Long narrow blossoms resemble honeysuckle on vigorous spreading plants. It is native in the southwestern deserts down into Baja proving its ability to survive long dry periods. This fuchsia is a rapid spreader that sends out aggressive underground roots that pop up new sprouts all around the original location. If conditions are right they can become downright invasive. Plants can become rangy if not cut back periodically with your hedge clippers. If planted in too much shade this perennial becomes quite leafy and may refuse to bloom. South facing locations are ideal.

Cuphea

Oenothera berlandieri | **Mexican Evening Primrose** | 12–18" tall, 2–3'wide | Despite its rock hard constitution, this primrose is the most feminine of all desert perennials. Three-inch wide cup flowers in a delicate shade of shell pink literally cover it for weeks in spring. You may find hummingbird moths around your evening primrose at dusk and dawn. These large, dark nocturnal fliers are its natural pollinators, as the pale blossoms are more easily seen in low light. This low growing perennial is among the fastest spreaders in the garden, its roots traveling through sandy soils to create large stands. They've been known to fill entire planters in just a few seasons. A native of Baja California, this primrose will take long dry periods in stride, but if adequately watered they flourish. After spring flowering, deadhead the entire stand to encourage more dense growth over the summer. The down side to this plant is that it blooms just a few weeks in spring. Plants self-sow in sandy soils providing plenty of volunteers to provide a truly remarkable carpet of delicate pink all by itself.

Oenothera berlandieri

GAZANIAS FOR MODERN HOMES

Any child of mid-century southern California can personally attest to the direct association of clumping gazanias with modern architecture. In the post-war era when so many of these houses were being built, the gazania breeders were coaxing a wide range of colors and exotic petal patterns from these South African daisies. The tidy clumps of foliage are topped with disproportionately large daisy blooms. They grow quite well in spring, but then, as now, consider these plants temporary. They tend to dwindle in vigor over about three years, then the plant dies out. Many will self-sow during that period to maintain a presence, but colors on these seedlings will be hit and miss. To maintain the traditional look, plant new individuals every year in the fall. Note: Do not confuse these clumpers with trailing forms that go by *Gazania leucolaena*.

Gazania

MEDIUM GROWERS

Penstemon eatonii | **Firecracker Penstemon** | 3' tall
Penstemon parryi | **Parry's Penstemon** | 4' tall
Penstemon superbus | **Coral Penstemon** | 5' tall | A single plant blooms at the curb edge of Sunrise Boulevard in the reflected heat and minimal water availability of that roadside site. It is a strange, exotic flower in the midst of a minimal dryland setting. Vivid orange red blossoms rise to nearly 4 feet, swaying with each passing car. This penstemon proves without question that success with these plants is all about drainage and full sun exposure. Best success is not in well-watered rich soil but in parsimonious desert earth with little to no fertilizer. The plant obviously liked to be located beside a curb where moisture is trapped and soil remains cooler beneath the paving. Similar conditions exist at edges of landscape boulders and patio slabs where they belong in home gardens. When in bloom these outstanding spikes are certainly tall plants, but for the rest of the season they are medium sized, and belong in the midst of these borders to ensure plenty of sun.

ABOVE LEFT: Pink penstemon hybrid
ABOVE RIGHT: *Penstemon parryi*

Encelia farinosa | **Brittlebush** | 3' tall, 4' wide | Sometimes we overlook the beauty of common things in favor of the exotic. Brittlebush is as common as dirt here, and when scattered across the desert with the creosote bush it lacks the appeal it has in the garden. Locally plentiful plants have made cottage gardens around the world unique to each locale, and this great plant is our desert garden signature. There is a superior source of great looking, greyish foliage that reflects the moonlight and defies the most extreme drought. Its woody trunk and branches produce a fine upright bushy character year-round. When they bloom in spring, the flower stalks topped with daisies are so abundant the entire plant turns bright yellow. If allowed to go to seed they will self-sow just as they do throughout the Coachella Valley. Capable of withstanding the most brutal drought, it is known to bloom out of season after a rain event. Plant at the edges of the cottage garden that tend to be too hot and dry, or so exposed it would wither any other candidate.

Encelea farinosa

Salvia farinacea

Penstemon fendleri

PENSTEMON AND SALVIA TREASURE TROVE

Two genera are responsible for a huge number of desert-hardy perennials and sub-shrubs. Consider these less common plants and their flower colors to augment what we've listed below.

Penstemon centranthifolius	**Scarlet Bugler**	Red
Penstemon fendleri	**Fendler Penstemon**	Purple
Penstemon superbus	**Coral Penstemon**	Red
Salvia chamaedryoides	**Blue Sage**	Blue
Salvia farinacea	**Mealycup Sage**	Blue

TALL GROWERS

Salvia leucantha | **Mexican Bush Sage** | 3–5' tall and wide

Soft and fuzzy yet big and burly describes the duality of this sage. Perennial only in the mildest parts of the state, it is coveted everywhere else. White fuzzy stems are wreathed in pinnate green-gray leaves and topped with spikes of purple flowers. No other Salvia can match it for speed to maturity nor overall visibility. But the real beauty of this sage is its resilient nature. It's this open casual transparency that can be most appealing in the cottage garden look. By the end of fall these plants can become rangy if not gently shaped during the growing season which sacrifices some blooms. Some gardeners prefer to cut the spring growth at a foot tall to encourage branching, which produces more densely held blooms. Remove all old stems when new ones appear at the base.

Ruellia penninsularis | **Baja Ruellia** | 3' tall, 2–3' wide | Blue is always the hardest color to get in desert plants. This Ruellia bears the most gorgeous, iridescent violet blue flowers. A fast growing heat lover, these tall rising perennials produce dark green stalks that are long blooming over much of the year. Though only a few flowers are open on the plant at any one time, they continue unabated most of the time. After plants go to seed the capsules pop open with an audible click to fling seed far and wide. This makes them potentially invasive in sandy soils where their strong underground stems can be tough to root out. It is best to keep the seedlings under control and the plants shaped nicely to produce a more garden-worthy form.

Ruellia penninsularis

Spaheralcea ambigua | **Globe Mallow** | 3' tall and wide

If you love old-fashioned hollyhocks, consider this the desert alternative. The globe mallow produces luscious orange flowers on plants just 3 feet tall with delightful upright spikes. You'll find wild versions of the species in the canyons surrounding the Coachella Valley where they bloom spectacularly in the spring. The rest of the year plants look like a bunch of scruffy sticks. In gardens this is a fast grower that won't take a great deal of water or it dies out. Keep in dry corners or edges where it receives plenty of sun. Like the penstemons, this perennial also prefers a large boulder nearby to rest upon and to root beneath. To renew plants after a couple of years, cut all stems to about 6 inches and allow them to grow out again. Some individuals, particularly seedlings may produce altered flower color through natural variability of the species, so be sure to buy in bloom to get the luscious orange color. Then once established, let it go to seed and see what shows up.

Spahaeralcea ambigua

Salvia farinacea

Leonotis leonurus | **Lions Tail** | 5–6' tall and wide | From the bush of inland South Africa comes a real looker that rivals southwestern plants with its drought resistance. It's a large, bushy, shrubby perennial, topped with rings of orange flowers in whorls amidst the dark green foliage. Growing much like the Mexican sage, it can become rangy with time and will stand a hard pruning for renewal. This is an exceptional dark green backgrounder that's a welcome relief from the typical silvery grey coloring of most desert plant foliage. You can expect continuous blooms from spring to the depths of winter followed by interesting seed capsules.

Antigonon leptopus | **Queen's Wreath Vine** | 10–20' long | This unique native of the Mexican desert produces bunches of delicate, coral red blossoms at the end of fast growing runners. It blooms nearly year-round except for the coldest winter days.

With time, the base of the plant becomes barren with growth at the tips. Hard pruning back to renew queen's wreath gives it a whole new look and life. With age a tuber-like caudex forms underground which holds water for use in dry spells. This romantic little beauty is cottage-garden perfect and may even self-sow. Adapted to dry washes it can put on surprisingly fast growth in the heat and celebrates the worst of our summer temperatures with flowers.

A queen's wreath vine allowed to invade a hedge of orange-flowered Cape honeysuckle and yellow *Tecoma stans* adds hot pink to the mix in the depths of summer.

LOCATION: PALO VERDE GARDEN CENTER

Hidden within the Living Desert is the little known Palo Verde Garden Center. It is without a doubt the best source of desert perennials in the region. Created to support the Living Desert with its profits, this small but intense nursery offers a fabulous selection of desert hardy plants. Many, but not all of these have been propagated at the Living Desert so they are naturally adapted to our low desert conditions. You can be sure that they grew up here from seed or cutting and will therefore have few transplant problems in their new locations.

Desert perennials are a true specialty. They are not carried by other retailers because of their unique preferences for soils, heat, and sun. But at Palo Verde there is a huge selection of salvias and penstemons for the perennial devotee as well as all of the other species included in this chapter. You'll also find some exceptional varieties of native shrubs, vines, and trees in smaller container sizes. Their selection of succulents is also world class, but note how much shade they are provided on display because many of these are grown in San Diego County and will need protection here. The best time to shop this garden center is during the winter months when it is fully stocked.

Palo Verde Garden Center at the Living Desert
47-900 Portola Avenue
Palm Desert, CA 92260
(760) 346-5694
http://www.livingdesert.org

Note: For shoppers, the garden center is accessible without paying the entry fee to the Living Desert.

THIS CHAPTER IN A NUTSHELL

1. Successful cottage gardens prefer morning sun with protection at midday and afternoon in the summer.

2. Plant both annuals and perennials for cottage gardens around October to maximize the adjustment period before new plants must face the summer heat.

3. Arrange plants for the cottage garden any way you wish provided the taller ones are behind shorter stature species so all receive equal sun and visibility.

4. Clumping hybrid gazanias were one of the favorite modern plants during the mid-century, and make excellent bright color accents for authentic restorations.

5. Native brittlebush and Mexican sage are two of the easiest and largest perennials for cottage gardens in the desert.

LOW DESERT NATIVES

The great illusion of the desert is that it appears barren, but there is life and beauty visible only to the keen eyed beholder. The truth is that the dry climate of the American Southwest and Mexico have produced some of the most elegant plants in the world. Many are succulent species while others are specially adapted to heat and drought through other means. These are all rugged individuals with strong architectural form and a wide range of textures that are bold tools in the hands of the designer. And for modern architecture they offer some of the most graphic landscape candidates.

Not long ago these species weren't widely available. With increased population in the desert southwest, the demand for hardy choices spurred supply through specialty growers. Limited water supply and environmental mandates have encouraged these plants further into the marketplace. What was once grown by specialists became stock and trade of large wholesale growers and their expanded distribution networks. Propagation of the plants in large quantities, like everything else, makes them more affordable.

This is a diverse lot. Each one has adapted some unique characteristic that helps it survive in the desert. Some are geared to rapid growth and flowering just after rainfall to take advantage of short-term moisture. One group reproduces, but only once in a single grand culminating event of its lifetime. Others have devised unique means of vegetative propagation to sustain the species in climates too dry to support seed germination. Each of these plants tells its own story, but somehow they all share an age-old dryland resonance.

Oddly enough, these desert dwellers can also be surprisingly water tolerant. Under abundant irrigation some grow faster and produce more blooms. The key is knowing how each one behaves. Most important is individual sun tolerance because many will scald here in full, unremitting summer exposures.

This chapter is divided into two parts. Part I features plants, often succulent, that grow in a rosette of leaves, and are appreciated primarily for their foliage which is attractive year-round. Some bloom each year, others do not. Part II groups a number of unique desert plants that offer flowers as well as a cast iron constitution.

PART I: ROSETTES

THE YUCCAS

The Joshua Tree is no stranger to the Coachella Valley, but you rarely see them grow below their optimal elevations in the high desert. Sure, there is an occasional specimen found around town and in botanical gardens, but in general the low desert is too dry for this species. They prefer the higher elevations where rainfall is more abundant and both summer and winter are cooler. You must work to establish a Joshua on the valley floor, and even then it's lifespan is not guaranteed.

The Joshua is just one species of the genus *Yucca*. This group within the lily family includes many species found across the southern United States and into Mexico.

What they all share is a unique relationship to moths that ensure pollination. The yucca then shelters the moth's young as they mature. It is one of the most famous symbiotic relationships of plant to animal in nature.

ABOVE LEFT: The newly forming bud of *Yucca brevifolia*, the Joshua tree.

BELOW LEFT: The Joshua tree of the high desert produces large waxy blossoms pollinated at night by a moth.

LEFT: Most yucca flowers hang downward during the day, then turn up to receive moths under the night sky.

When the yucca blooms, it cannot be pollinated by the bees that flock to its flowers because the pollen is too wet and sticky. But at night the flowers emit a nocturnal fragrance and may even change their orientation to the night sky. This combined with their white coloring reflects moonlight so perfectly that it lures this special moth with light and scent. The female moth will deposit her eggs in the ovary of the flower, then roll a ball of pollen to stuff into the opening, sealing off the young inside the waxy womb. Larvae soon hatch and consume some developing seeds, but never all of them. There is enough viable seed remaining to sustain the yucca.

Garden designers know all too well how fabulous yucca flowers appear in a moonlit desert landscape. Too often they are located out of view when they should be front and center around outdoor living areas. Only when outdoors and not faded by interior lights will the true luminescence of the yucca bloom reveal itself.

Yucca elata | **Soaptree Yucca** | 10–20' tall | Single or multiple head
Resembling a young Joshua tree, this is a fine upstanding form that offers a big bold accent with fine-textured foliage. Spectacular white flowers bloom on stalks up to 6 feet tall for a really showy accent night or day. The common name arises from the natural saponifiers present in its roots that were used by Native American tribes within its range in the high deserts of New Mexico and Arizona.

Yucca baccata | **Datil Yucca** | 3–4' tall | Multiple head | A California native that can be seen in the high desert growing in Joshua Tree National Park, it tends to spread into colonies by underground stems producing bluish clumps of foliage. Flower stalks are also uniquely colored by flower buds wrapped in purplish-brown covers. This plant is quite similar to soaptree yucca, but the leaves are smoother and it is better adapted to the low desert. Large fleshy fruits were an important food crop of Native American tribes.

Yucca elata

Yucca rostrata | **Beaked Yucca** | 8–12' tall | Single head |

This is an exceptional Mexican species featuring a single spherical foliage head atop a single trunk. Its architectural form makes it outstanding for mid-century modern and desert modern homes. A single, tall flower head rises from the center in spring. Slow growth makes specimen plants costly.

Yucca recurvifolia | **Recurved Yucca** | 4–6' tall | Short trunk |

While this yucca grows quite well in the desert, it is not as capable of withstanding the dry climate due to its nativity in the southeastern states. It is also the only yucca considered vulnerable to snout weevil. Colored cultivars with yellow leaves and variegation are popular among modern designers, but the vulnerability to pests should be considered before planting in ground.

Yucca shidigera | **Mojave Yucca** | 6–12' tall | Short trunk |

This is another yucca found in the Joshua tree plant community of the high desert. Not as attractive as other yuccas due to its dense shrubby form, it's not cultivated as often. Thick flower heads resembling that of Joshua trees sit tightly in the foliage rather than above it as with other yuccas. Ideal for all native and wildlife gardens due to large fruit that is attractive to many species. It is also consumed by Cahuilla Indians living within its range.

ABOVE LEFT: *Yucca rostrata*

LEFT: *Yucca recurvifolia*

THE NOTORIOUS AGAVE SNOUT WEEVIL

Cruise the very old neighborhoods of Palm Springs and Palm Desert and you are unlikely to find a single large agave in those landscapes. This is explained by a single pest, the weevil, that singlehandedly wipes out valley agaves large and small. The first sign of a problem is meltdown, when normally upstanding leaves gradually lie down leaving only the central cone in upright position. This symptom is often mistaken for dehydration until closer inspection reveals the fact that plants are no longer anchored to the ground. A gentle tug reveals a succulent core, brown with rot and infested with big, white grub worms. These tunnel through the center of the plant severing connections between root and leaf.

"That's why you don't see agave nurseries out here," says Clark Moorten who was born in the valley. "Every few years we get a bad weevil infestation that devastates the agaves." This problem isn't unique to this desert. It is the age-old affliction of the blue agave of Mexico, from which tequila is made. The worm in the bottom of the bottle is the grub of the agave snout weevil.

Agave snout weevils strike in the heat of the summer. Adult weevils burrow their hard snouts into the flesh of the central cone of unfurled leaves leaving an isolated but visible brown spot. They release a bacteria into the plant tissues that rapidly spreads through the succulent cells rendering them much easier for the grubs to consume. Then it lays eggs in the hole. Once the grubs hatch out they begin eating tunnels down through the center of the plant. When they reach the soil they'll leave the dying or dead agave plant and pupate in the earth. Once weevils have made a home in your soil it is difficult, if not impossible to control them without heavy chemicals.

Weevils seem to prefer the blue *Agave americana* and its variegated sibling, but virtually all species are vulnerable. However, some individual agave plants have proven inexplicably resistant. In the wild these will be the only ones to survive the weevils, their equally resistant offspring able to preserve the species from utter devastation. If you find a very old agave in the valley with a lot of pups, it's probably a genetically resistant individual. The pups will be genetically resistant too. Sever them from the root and transplant into your garden.

The long nose of this weevil is perfectly adapted to pierce the central stem of the agave plant.

The adult weevil is a beetle that lays her eggs within the agave flesh, which hatch into voracious grubs that tunnel through the core of the plant, then pupate in the soil.

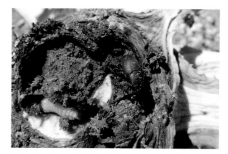

Grubs have killed this agave by consuming all the tissues that link the roots to the above ground portion.

THE AGAVES

The agave is the biggest no-brainer of the succulent world. There are over 150 species native to the Americas, and many of these have become vital commodities to the cultures that depend on them. Agave is the source of tequila, sisal fibers used to make rope, and many other useful items in Latin America. They are the Western Hemisphere equivalent to the aloes of southern Africa.

The commodities of the agave are derived from the ground-dwelling rosette of foliage that unlike the yucca, does not produce a trunk. As insurance that the species survives, the rosette will produce smaller offsets around its base called "pups," that can strike their own roots over time. Severing pups is the primary way agaves are propagated.

Each species flowers at the end of its designated life span, which can vary anywhere from ten to fifty years. Only the mother plant blooms and dies. Eventually each of the pups will flower too, surrounded by their own crop of pups. In the wild, agaves can create colonies of various aged individuals, but the DNA of each one will be identical.

ABOVE LEFT: Although recently planted, this *Agave desmettiana* is flowering because it has reached the designated reproductive age of this species.

ABOVE RIGHT: Agaves flower just once in their life span and then die shortly after.

LEFT: This *Agave media-picta* has produced dozens of pups or offsets around its base to replace the mother plant after it blooms and dies.

All agaves spend their life preparing for a single, grand reproductive act before they die. During its life the agave produces a head of foliage that works to gather energy in its tissues. It will need all this food to bolt into a stalk and flower at life's end. When an agave bolts, the spaces between the tightly packed leaves elongate into stems that rise into a tall spire of blooms. These can be a single, enormous pole topped with blossoms or may be branched high up with separate clusters of golden blossoms. These are so rich in nectar that the agave blooms are favored by hummingbirds, bees, bats, and a variety of other insects.

Some agaves utilize yet another vegetative technique to ensure survival. Where climates are very dry, agave seed may have little chance to germinate. Therefore the bloom stalk itself will produce pups, hundreds of them around the flowers on a single plant. As the stalk finally dies, the pups fall to earth and root into new genetically-identical plants. All around the Coachella Valley are examples of bloom spire pups that can be gathered and planted into whole gardens for free.

Easy to grow, great looking agave species have proven their worth in the desert landscape. However, many more will grow here with varying levels of protection from the sun. Those listed below are the most favored for landscaping or in containers, and are widely available. Difficulty in obtaining large plants of other species may be due to their lack of provenance in our Coachella Valley climate.

Many agaves produce small pups on their flower stalks, which can be plucked and rooted easily in ground or pots.

Agave angustifolia | 3–5' rosette |
Grown for centuries as a fiber agave, this rounded form produces variegated leaves that are highly attractive and resilient in the desert heat. It has proven to be weevil resistant and many very old plants can be seen throughout established neighborhoods and street plantings around the valley.

Agave angustifolia

Agave deserti

This is an exceedingly rare example of a monstrose agave spike found in local roadside landscaping.

Agave deserti | 2' rosette | This is the only agave native to California. Wild specimens can be seen along the most treacherous parts of Highway 74 in the Carizzo Road area above Palm Desert. This location underscores the importance of drainage to this species which may not survive in irrigated landscapes. They bear wide leaves in a lovely shade of blue-gray with occasional greener-colored individuals. Incredibly resistant to heat, drought, and rocky ground, they are an exceptional choice for problem soils of cove communities and mesas along the south rim of the valley.

Agave desmettiana | 3' rosette | This species is beloved by designers who appreciate the unique, lotus flower-like form of this agave. Deep bluish-green leaves rise in a precise vase shape that widens at the top with a graceful little flip. They take on their best appearance as juveniles because most will begin producing large quantities of pups later in life making them shrubby looking. During the freeze of 2006–07, these agaves were singed but not killed by frost. Good examples in full sun can be seen at the Wellness Park on the corner of Tachevah and Miraleste across from Desert Regional Hospital in Palm Springs.

Agave geminiflora | 2–3' rosette | This is a unique, fine-textured agave with 100 to 200 stiff, wickedly pointed leaves in a single ground-hugging rosette. Small size and exceptional symmetry make it a favorite among modern designers, and it is absolutely stellar in containers. It may be difficult to handle and dangerous to children due to the sheer number of stiff needle-like points. This quality makes these agave theftproof and more weevil resistant.

Agave vilmorniana | **Octopus Agave** | 3–5' rosette | Visit The Gardens on El Paseo in Palm Desert and you'll see just how beautiful this sun-tolerant agave can be. They are also found commonly in median and commercial building landscapes. Large, open and sinuous, these plants are tough and manage to survive weevils to some extent, but are not considered resistant. They look best when planted in groups to compound their mass. This agave produces pups on its flower stalks.

OTHER AGAVE SPECIES KNOWN TO THRIVE IN THE COACHELLA VALLEY

Agave bovicornuta

Agave guiengola

Agave lechugilla

Agave macrocantha

Agave parryi

Agave parviflora

Agave sisalana

Agave victoriae-reginae

Agave vilmorniana

ABOVE LEFT: *Agave sisalana*

ABOVE: *Agave parryi*

LEFT: *Agave lechugilla*

Hesperaloe parviflora

Dasilirion longissimum

Hesperaloe parviflora | **Red Yucca** | 3–4' tall, and over 6' wide | This is a rare, bright bloomer in the rosette foliage crowd. A native of the Sonoran desert, it grows in upright clumps that spread by underground stems into masses over 6 feet wide. When out of bloom it greatly resembles a grassy aloe, but the bloom spikes are what distinguishes its beauty. Plants bloom each year over a very long season extending from spring to fall. They produce tall stalks bearing delicious cream and coral colored tubular flowers, although cultivars of wholly creamy yellow and true red flowers are available. They are outstanding hummingbird nectar sources. Some really excellent masses of both colors can be seen in the median planting of Gene Autry Trail just east of the Palm Springs Airport.

Dasilirion wheeleri | **Desert Spoon** | 5' tall and 7' wide | The desert spoon produces a beautiful sky-blue rosette of incredible size. Later in life it will develop a short trunk, raising the height of the foliage up to 7 feet at maturity. It's a tough-as-nails plant capable of surviving abandoned commercial sites. What makes this plant so useful is not only the fact that it grows just about anywhere, but it also produces truly majestic 12-foot-tall flower spikes each year. Though the blooms are not colorful, they present a strong architectural form. Cut them when dry to use decoratively indoors and out.

Dasilirion longissimum | **Mexican Grass Tree** | 5' tall and wide | The fine texture of this remarkable species is in big demand for modern architecture. Fine 1/4-inch-wide leaves are arrayed in a perfect hemisphere around the center of the plant similar to a contemporary metallic sculpture. For best results, locate them clear of any other plant that might crowd it and thus spoil the perfect symmetry. A tough Mexican native that does best with some shade and with regular water will grow far more quickly.

Nolina microcarpa | **Bear Grass** | You'll find examples of native *Nolina* growing in Chino Canyon on the road up to the Palm Springs Tram. It loves lower levels of north-facing, rocky, well-drained slopes where it can grow protected from hot sun by the canyon walls. Despite the common name, it is not a grass but a member of the agave family. In the wild it produces dense but irregular forms. In the landscape it takes on a more symmetrical shape, with white or greenish blooms atop a 2-foot stem held close above the leaves. This is a great native for wild gardens and solves problems for hillside homes with extreme drainage and poor fertility.

PART II: WOODY PLANTS AND SUBSHRUBS

Fouquieria splendens | **Ocotillo** | 15' tall, 10' wide | This is perhaps the most easily identified native of the California desert. They can be seen in the wild along the eastern access to Joshua Tree National Park off Highway 10 and up on Highway 74 near Pinyon Crest. Many old ocotillos can be seen in residential landscapes around the valley growing adjacent to lawns as well as in very dry settings. This illustrates the wide range of adaptability of the ocotillo. In fact, ocotillo can leaf out and go deciduous again many times within the span of the year in response to rainfall. An old trick to coaxing them into leaf is to spray the plants after sunset in the heat of the summer, which mimics the monsoonal cloudbursts of Arizona.

These unique plants are woody, with tall rod-like branches arranged in a very sculptural vase shape. Spring blooms occur in large flames of bright red blossoms at the branch tips. Most ocotillos sold today are bare roots ripped out of the Arizona desert. This causes incredible stress to the plants and they require a long time to become established. Resist the temptation to select the largest bare root, for these will have the greatest stress damage. Younger specimens will adapt to transplanting and become established far more quickly. Those grown in containers may prove to be the most vigorous.

Nolina microcarpa

Fouquieria splendens

THE SMOKE TREE

It's rare to see a smoke tree anywhere but in a dry wash. Unless you're a hiker, you're unlikely to see *Dalea spinosa* up close. An occasional old specimen may be found in dry home landscapes around the valley.

What residents and visitors rarely see is the smoke tree's exquisite iridescent indigo flowers. The small but intensely-colored blooms open in the heat of summer when few venture out onto the simmering desert floor. The blossoms are produced so heavily the wispy foliage sags under the weight. Bees flock to them in droves. The fallen flowers create a blue carpet around the base of every plant.

Smoke trees are difficult if not impossible to grow. In the wild they spring up after rain events from seed washed down through the gravel. Under these conditions they produce a tap root to reach deep moisture, then grow like weeds. One wide drainage way in Cathedral City is packed with nothing but adolescent smoke trees. Rarely will you find a young one in cultivation or for sale except perhaps at the Living Desert Garden Center or other native specialty nurseries. They are devilishly difficult to transplant, so if you are fortunate enough to be blessed with a smoke tree in your yard, consider it a rare and wonderful gift.

Calliandra californica | **Baja Fairy Duster** | 4' tall and wide
A profusion of Christmas-red powder-puff blossoms give the
fairy dusters a delightful, almost whimsical look in the garden.
The blooms are actually a bundle of stamens that prove irresistible
to hummingbirds. But don't let its small fern-like foliage fool you,
for this is a rough, tough native that's most attractive when left to its
natural open form. Unfortunately it is too often clipped into a dense
mass, sacrificing its open airy character which better enhances the
visibility of the flowers. This species is found in Baja California and
is therefore more frost sensitive than its locally native cousin.

Calliandra eriophylla | **Fairy Duster** | 3' tall, 4' wide | This
California native is nearly identical to the Baja fairy duster except its
flowers are pink. The coloring may be more appealing for a softer
cottage garden color palette. But what really separates the two is
that this local native is far more frost hardy, to as low as 15°F. This
is a more reliable species, particularly in low lying sites of the east
valley with abnormally cold winters.

Justica californica | **Chuparosa** | 3' tall, 4' wide | Translated
from the Spanish, *chuparosa* means "sucking rose," which describes
its bright red flowers that appeal to hummingbirds. Good examples
can be seen along hiking trails throughout the valley in the early
spring when blooming bright red among the wildflowers. They
thrive in the open where there is plenty of air movement because
plants can be damaged by mild frost. Compromise its direct sunlight
and plants may not bloom at all. This rugged native is a bold spring
accent in very dry gardens, but may seem far too rangy for small
landscapes. They're ideal in wide open spaces in association with
cacti, ocotillo, and ornamental grasses.

Calliandra californica

Calliandra eriophylla

Cassia artemisioides

Cassia artemisioides | **Feathery Cassia or Senna** | 6' tall | While many species of Cassia are grown in desert gardens, this group is evergreen and thus provides a more suitable year-round candidate. Outstanding golden yellow blooms cover these desert-hardy shrubs in the winter and spring. Very drought resistant, they can stand alone in the dryland desert garden, but under irrigation they become even more lush and can adapt well to a traditional setting. Light grey-green needle-like foliage provides an excellent neutral background for outdoor living spaces without sacrificing air movement. Brownish pods follow the flowers. If pods are removed the plants remain far more attractive. Note: Some references list these plants under genus *Senna*, others under *Cassia* so consider them interchangeable. This evergreen species features three different closely related options:

Senna artemisioides; Feathery Cassia

Senna artemisioides, subspecies *filifolia;* Bushy Senna

Senna artemisioides, subspecies *petiolaris;* Desert Senna

LOCATION: THE LIVING DESERT

This incredible zoological garden is a relative newcomer, as are most things you find in the Coachella Valley. It began as a philanthropic effort to protect the flora and fauna of the desert through public education. Local residents were concerned that rapid growth would reduce appreciation for the fragile habitat the desert provides for so many different species.

In 1970, private donors in conjunction with the Desert Museum set aside 360 acres in Palm Desert as an interpretive nature trail through a living preserve of desert plants and animals. In the mid-1970s, creation of both high and low desert habitats was achieved featuring full plant communities. With a great deal of land to work with, designers of these "gardens" have truly recreated the look and feel of the wild desert in a smaller controlled location. This allows visitors to see the natives up-close and personal with their natural companion plants, just as they would be in more remote wildlands. Over the years the Living Desert has become fully independent and has expanded to include plants and animals from dry regions around the world.

For gardeners, the Living Desert botanical plantings are the best way to become familiar with local natives ideal for landscaping. They feature the full range of trees, shrubs, perennials, wildflowers, cacti, and succulents from North America, which includes Mexico. All the plants are well labeled so identification is easy. The convenient location lets you visit the Living Desert at various times of year to see how a plant may look in winter and summer, wet years and dry.

If you find the gardens daunting in their sheer size, magnitude, and diversity, consider taking a guided tour. For those more serious about desert gardening, courses at the Living Desert University are world-class educational experiences that will tell you far more about all the natives described in this book.

To learn more, log on to the Living Desert website at http://www.livingdesert.org . Included in the expansive site are up-to-date schedules of events at the zoological gardens as well as class schedules at Living Desert University.

The Living Desert
47-900 Portola Avenue
Palm Desert, CA 92260
(760) 346-5694

THIS CHAPTER IN A NUTSHELL

1. The tall white bloom stalks of yucca are designed by nature to reflect and magnify moonlight to attract a certain moth, its only pollinator.

2. Agaves are afflicted with snout weevil, a pest that periodically decimates the valley's agave population; *Agave angustifolia* appears to be the only resistant species.

3. Agaves bloom only once in their lives while yucca, desert spoon, and bear grass bloom annually.

4. When buying ocotillo bare root, choose a small one because these adjust to new locations better than larger, older plants.

5. Some agave bloom stalks bear pups, which are identical copies of the parent plant that can be plucked off, planted, and quickly strike roots.

CHAPTER 8

THE TROPICALS

Peek over the walls of Old Las Palmas and you'll find living proof that Palm Springs is a tropical desert. Banana trees, hibiscus, and plumeria, all of South Pacific origin thrive here, but only if properly located to protect from wind and occasional frost. It's just this tropical look that gave the village of Palm Springs its unique character. The protective influence of the steep Mt. San Jacinto escarpment created a climatically protected enclave unlike anywhere else in the valley.

In the early years of Palm Springs, architecture was largely Spanish colonial, with thick walls, red tile roofs, and broad verandas. Even today many adobe brick homes are inhabited throughout the Movie Colony. Before the desert natives were fully appreciated, these homes featured plants that epitomized the southern California lifestyle with its tropical plants and vivid flowers. Perhaps more important was the fragrance, redolent of citrus and jasmine, that filled the night air of these old homes.

Today these same tropical plants can be used to create truly wonderful fantasy landscapes. The surge of the Tommy Bahama island style has blended with these old Spanish style homes to create a more contemporary tropical palette. Combined with landscape palms from chapter 2, these blooming beauties can create a truly magical environment.

It's essential to understand the limitations of tropicals. Most evolved in a far more humid climate with heavy moisture that filters UV rays. While tropicals can take the heat, they are challenged by the desert's dry air and thin atmosphere. The plants will languish if not protected and sufficiently watered to compensate for moisture loss.

Wind is their greatest danger. It is capable of drawing moisture out of large leaves at an alarming rate. Wind can tatter the foliage of tropical plants, creating splits through which even more moisture is lost. This kind of damage shreds the leaves, browning the edges around the wounds.

Tropicals are fare of protected courtyards and the lee sides of buildings, but some areas may not be able to support them at all. Homes in the center of the valley's "wind belt" may prove all too hostile for this group. Those sequestered in coves of the mountains where they are protected may find remarkable success with very little effort. Suffice to say that tropicals are wholly environmentally driven plants, and you either have the right conditions for them or you don't.

Strelitzia reginae | **Bird of Paradise** | *Strelitzia nicolai* | **Giant Bird of Paradise**

The signature flower of the exotic tropical look in the 1930s was the bird of paradise, and it remains so today. This large leaf perennial is a native of southern Africa where it tolerates very high temperatures in the dry season. That is why it does well in Palm Springs in wind-protected locations, provided it receives adequate water to produce frequent new leaves. They are almost never seen out in the open. Although they thrive in full sun just a few miles west, birds are burned beyond recognition in the desert due to extreme moisture loss. Therefore above all, it is protection that allows these fabulous flowers to grow here.

This goes double for the much larger giant bird of paradise with its less colorful boat-shaped flowers. Like the bananas discussed later in this chapter, the large leaves can present a problem for tattering, burn, and moisture loss. Stems may not be strong enough to resist bending as the large leaves are pushed like giant sails by wind. These beauties have found a home in large estate home atriums or very tall-ceiling outdoor living rooms where they are fully protected. Nothing matches their tropical beauty for rendering too much hard stucco and concrete into a lush tropical paradise.

Strelitzia reginae

Beaucarnea recurvata | **Ponytail Palm** | The genus *Beaucarnea* translates to "beautiful flesh," describing the swollen base or caudex of the trunk that serves as water storage tissue. One or more main trunks rise out of the base, topped with foliage that is palm-like, but not related to palms at all. The *Beaucarneas* originate in Mexico and are remarkably heat and drought resistant. In ground or in pots, they are sculptural plants that deserve to be positioned as focal points. Be aware that beaucarnea are vulnerable to direct afternoon sun in the summer and will require protection. Damage to the bark of the caudex can become an avenue by which moisture may enter and begin terminal rot. If injured, withhold water to allow the wound to thoroughly callus before irrigating.

Strelitzia nicolai

MO TIPS
In winter, air warmed during the day will rise into the night sky to be replaced by cold air sliding down off the mountains. Warmth beneath a tree canopy is prevented from freely rising, so it remains trapped there. Conditions here will be a few degrees warmer in the morning than on open ground. It will be even warmer under solid patio covers. Keep your marginally-hardy tropicals in these locations to reduce frost damage. If a severe frost is expected, drape a bedsheet over the plants for added protection. Never drape with plastic.

This old stand of *Sanseveria trifasciata*, a relic of this mid-modern original, has completely filled in this linear planter.

The sanseveria in the pot on the left has cracked its container and is spreading over the rim via thick fleshy roots

Sanseveria trifasciata | **Mother In Law Tongue**

This is the signature plant of the mid-century home relegated to indoor planting everywhere but Palm Springs. It is also a popular plant in tropical Mexico, where it is grown in rustic terra cotta pots. Plants are valued for their long sword-like foliage which remains green year-round.

The popular yellow-striped and margined form is well known, but a dozen cultivars in varying shades of green provide more options in the garden. Height also ranges from dwarfs just 6 inches tall, to 4-foot-tall forms.

This foliage thrives in surprisingly low light without leaning toward the illumination source. It produces fine texture and rigid geometry on top of a highly drought-resistant nature. Thick rhizomes (underground roots), produce upright sprouts at intervals allowing them to fill pots and planters in no time. These are easy to divide into new plants by severing sections of the rhizome with sprouts. Protect from frost and keep dry in winter.

In recent years other lesser-known species primarily from Madagascar have burst onto the scene with the modern movement's demand for plants. *Sanseveria cylindrica* is the most sought-after form. Three-foot long perfectly round leaves are produced in a symmetrical fan shape. A very dwarf form of this is just a foot tall.

ARCHITECTURAL TROPICALS IN CONTAINERS

For owners of estate homes, the ability to grow large architectural plants in containers is perfect for instant décor. Containers may be moved around, repotted, or replaced for a fresh look each new season. Pots featuring large tropical-looking plants can make versatile centerpieces for ever-changing seasonal color.

Custom combinations that carefully reflect the overall decorating scheme can enhance indoor-outdoor spaces like nothing else. When bullet spotlights or uplights are incorporated into these master potted works, it turns them into living art after dark. While not necessarily economical, the specimen plants may be changed periodically to improve or alter the effect along with evolving décor. Moller's Garden Center in Palm Desert is the valley's premier source of this kind of tropical container art.

When a garden is designed with containers to hold tropical plants, these tender species can be more easily moved or changed out with the season.

Hibiscus rosa-sinensis | **Hibiscus** | Few plants rival hibiscus for its large, intensely-colored flowers that signify the South Pacific like no other. Old specimens can be found in Palm Springs, but these are almost always in tight spaces or under protection of veranda, eaves, or tree canopies. They feature only a few colors— red, pink, or white. Occasional cold morning frost, and in particular the freeze of 2006–07, wreaked havoc on hibiscus planted in the open since the last frost of that magnitude had been decades prior.

ABOVE: *Carissa grandiflora*
BELOW: *Canna indica 'Phaison'*

Only those individuals with significant protection survived. This proves that if you want to invest in hibiscus, be sure they are in a sheltered locale. The fact that established hibiscus in the valley are usually single color blossoms without any of the flushes and frills points to the fact that the fancy hybrids may have lost some of their resiliency with breeding. They may be far more vulnerable to extremes of heat and cold. Even though these fancy hybrids are sold here, it doesn't mean they are sustainable in the desert.

Carissa grandiflora | **Natal Plum** | They are native to the northwestern corner of South Africa, mainly in the province of Natal. The thorns and thick fleshy leaves solve problems brought on by browsing wildlife and moisture loss from drought, heat, and wind. What is too often unappreciated about these dark green, lush shrubs is their intensely fragrant flowers that rival the scent of plumeria. Sadly, Carissa is too often clipped and sheared, preventing the flowers from forming. Following the white, inch-wide, star-shaped blooms are fruits that turn bright red at maturity. They are edible and commonly consumed in Africa. The species has yielded a number of cultivars in varying sizes that allow greater adaptability to small gardens—the full dwarf form 'Tomlinson' (2' by 3'); slightly larger 'Tuttle' (3' by 5'); and superior-fruiting 'Fancy' (6' by 6'), offer perfectly-sized choices for any size garden.

Canna indica 'Phaison' | **Tropicanna** | The old world of grandmother's cannas was recently revolutionized by the introduction of Tropicanna with its incredibly striped purple-maroon leaves. These plants have swept the national marketplace as signatures of the tropical and modern garden. Viewed as both a foliage and flower producer, their tall forms are excellent contrast in a lush landscape. When backlit by the morning sun they are true standouts in winter. Be aware that these plants have problems because they require direct sun and yet are burned by our intense UV light in summer. If planted in shade they languish and fail to stand up straight. Therefore they're best planted in containers that can be moved around with the seasons. The recent introduction of Tropicanna Gold and Tropicanna Black has produced some truly exceptional plants that can transform a garden, pool area, or outdoor living space in an instant. But don't be surprised if it fails to thrive in future seasons unless provided the perfect location.

Macfadyena unguis-cati | **Cats Claw Creeper** | Until recently the entire south side of the Mizell Senior Center in Palm Springs was completely covered with this creeper. A self-clinging tropical vine, it bursts into bloom in spring, turning the entire building lemon-yellow. Blossoms are tropical trumpet flowers that invite hummingbirds in droves. The vine was recently pulled down to allow painting of the building, and no stucco damage resulted because this plant clings by tiny suction cup holdfasts. They don't enter the masonry and thus are safer than most. This example also indicates the preferred exposure, on south-facing walls, fences and slopes.

Passiflora alato-caereulea | **Passion Flower Vine** | Fast-growing and borderline rampant, passion vines just love the desert. They produce one of the most complex flowers of the plant kingdom. Passion vines bloom prodigiously in an incredible shade of violet and purple with exquisite details. This makes them exceptional choices for close-up viewing, but beware of their eventual size. Runner tips continue to grow and flower, leaving the base of the vine bare and unattractive. This is a larval food plant for a certain butterfly which lays its eggs on the leaves. When larvae hatch out they devour the vine and cause a mess. The larvae may also infest other plants nearby. For the wildlife lover looking forward to seeing the birds decimate the larvae, or for anyone who finds this flower irresistible, they'll have great success with all types of passion vines in the desert. Just beware of the butterflies and prepare to be overwhelmed.

ABOVE: *Macfadyena unguis-cacti*
BELOW: *Passiflora alato-caereulea*

Rosa banksia | **Lady Banks Rose** | Even in the world of roses, this is a unique species. Evergreen and thornless, it is more of a vine than a rose. It is exceptional for arching over gateways or cloaking a chain-link fence with pleasing foliage and flowers. The plants bloom in spring with a load of small white or yellow highly fragrant blossoms, each about the size of a quarter. There is a good example of this species in Palm Springs on a chain link fence at the O'Donnel Golf Course just behind the Hyatt Hotel at Palm Canyon Boulevard.

**WARNING:
MORNING GLORY**

For those moving to the desert from northern climates, the beauty of morning glory may be irresistible. Elsewhere these tropical vines may be cut back by autumn frost, killing it entirely. But here in the desert these plants survive the winter and keep growing year-round, rooting as their runners travel. Once established it can be very difficult to eradicate, particularly if it infests other plantings. Toxic morning glory sap can also be absorbed by human skin. Do yourself a favor and pass by the morning glories at the garden center.

Hippeastrum vittatum | **Amaryllis** | The great red amaryllis flowers so admired as greenhouse or interior flowering bulbs are exceptional outdoor garden flowers in the desert. They are a fully tropical plant and virtually all those you buy for interiors will make fine garden flowers in Palm Springs. The most well proven are the bright red sorts with white throats, but today's options include white, coral, pink, and some truly exotic color combinations. Bulbs grow and bloom in shade or sun, but to prevent leaf scorch, protect them from direct afternoon sun and hot wind in summer. Like all bulbs, these plants will produce offsets and may be divided periodically, otherwise they will expand into large colonies.

Bananas | Now and then an old stand of banana rises above the fence line of someone's yard. These plants can be very old with many pseudostems that rise out of an ever-expanding mass of thick roots. But consider this a rare occurrence and note the number of tears in the edges of each of the long banana tree leaves. They make the otherwise wide leaves hang thin and listless from the central spine. This is wind damage and moisture loss. In slightly colder climates frost kills the stems back in the winter when plants look horrible for months, only to grow again in early summer. Here, bananas nipped by frost will be at their worst in high season. Unless you're prepared to look at winter damage while nurturing them in exactly the right location, this may not be a wise choice for desert gardens.

Ficus nitida | **Hedge Fig** | In the past twenty years, this fast-growing, bright green tree has been utilized for privacy screens. It is the primary replacement for ailing oleander. They surround many front yards to create private entries where city codes prevent tall boundary walls. Some truly monumental examples surround old Movie Colony estates with massive trunks hidden beneath the foliage. This is a clue to the true nature of these trees, which can reach up to 50 feet if allowed to grow naturally.

Commercial growers of Ficus hedge stock produce plants in staked columnar forms that are typically lined up into tightly spaced hedges. Over time these will encounter difficulties of invasive roots and overcrowded trunks which will crack wall foundations and raise sidewalks just as this same Ficus has done along the coast in Newport Beach. In the winter of 2006–07 we saw another weakness of these plants when they were burned back by frost all over Palm Springs. Some younger individuals died outright. But for sheer beauty, color, and form, the fig hedge is still alive and well as the living fence of favor in Palm Springs.

The lush tropical feel of the above composition depends strictly on foliage, while those to the right create a lush green backdrop for bright tropical blooms.

WHAT MAKES A LANDSCAPE LOOK TROPICAL?

You might be surprised to discover it's not necessarily flowers that make a tropical garden. What makes it so appealing in the desert is the presence of green. The wild jungle or rainforest is for the most part a collection of green foliage plants that produce unusually large leaves. When contrasting shades of green and leaf textures play against one another, you get a lush appearance with a cooling effect. It also creates a background against which you can arrange colorful flowering plants, furniture, art, and night lighting. Creating a surrounding "jungle" of foliage is a practical way to control sun and wind as well as absorbing glare from adjacent buildings and rooftops.

Cyperus papyrus

Cyperus papyrus | Papyrus | This beauty of the Egyptian desert is a fabulous choice for creating exotic gardens in our desert. Papyrus is a marginal plant—reeds that grow at the edges or "margins" of waterways that rise and fall with the season. When the Nile is high the papyrus flourish, growing lush and green in dense colonies. As the water recedes in the dry season the plants die back, turn brown, and dry out. The root remains alive in the muck waiting for waters to rise again. For this reason it's tough to grow papyrus here as a terrestrial plant, like in Los Angeles. They dry out so fast there isn't enough soil water to replenish the stalks. But if you grow them as if the Nile was in full flood mode by submerging their nursery container inside a large, decorative ceramic pot full of water, they will happily last throughout the summer season. Keep the water level above that of the nursery pot at all times and use nontoxic "mosquito dunks" from the garden center or mosquito fish to prevent larvae. Be aware that the stalks can be bent in half by wind, so protect these wispy beauties within sheltered courtyards and on the lee sides of buildings.

NO NEW ZEALAND FLAX

The fabulously-colored cultivars of *Phormium tenax*, a New Zealand sword-leaf plant used to perfection in Los Angeles, is a no-go in the desert. While it may tolerate drought inland, it melts down in the high heat of the desert summer. As a winter accent for indoor-outdoor architectural pots, they make fine temporary specimens.

THE KEY TO MID-CENTURY DESIGN: ROBERTO BURLE MARX

Roterto Burle Marx entered the fine art world as the modern movement was in full swing. A native of Brazil and raised among lovers of the native flora, his interests were divided between modern art and gardening. At some point the two came together making this famous designer the most important landscape architect for the modern architectural movement. His works in São Paulo and Copacabana Beach defined a ground plane and plants like a modern painting, and produced some of the most incredible landscapes in the world. Many books have been written about his landscapes, and those interested in the modern garden as it relates to mid-century modern architecture in Palm Springs will find the answers they crave among these heavily illustrated pages. Do not forget that there are no new ideas, only the applications change. So rather than recreate the wheel with mid-century makeovers, take a design lesson from Marx.

LOCATION: MOLLER'S GARDEN CENTER, PALM DESERT

Hidden in a box canyon at the base of the mountain in Palm Desert is the valley's most important retail garden center. This full-service operation offers the best selection of plants for landscaping, a vast array of garden art and fountains, specimen plants, and the best of the bougainvilleas both full-sized and dwarf. Their citrus inventory is unsurpassed. Here you'll find the most complete range of perennials and annual bedding plants as well as rabbit-proof geraniums. This is the best place in town to find exceptional ornamental grasses and shade plants for courtyards and atriums. They offer bold specimen-size desert plants for instant landscaping options.

Moller's also features an elegant interiors shop with contemporary décor items and realistic artificial flowers and succulent plants for indoor use. The florist is known valley-wide. Plant artisans create huge color bowls, overflowing hanging baskets, and mammoth planted centerpieces for gardens. Their selection of houseplants is unmatched in beauty, diversity, and sheer size.

With decades here in the valley, the Moller family has made their garden center ground zero for everything plant and garden related. However, due to the difficulty of keeping nursery plants in the extreme heat, their inventory is vastly reduced in the summer months, and is replenished by early fall in preparation for the October planting rush. It is too often overlooked on Painter's Path, just to the west of the Desert Crossing Shopping Center at Fred Waring Boulevard.

Moller's Garden Center
72-235 Painter's Path | Palm Desert, CA 92260
Nursery: (760) 346-0545 | Flower shop: (760) 346-9415
www.mollersgarden.com

THIS CHAPTER IN A NUTSHELL

1 The hallmark of the tropical garden is a liberal use of lush greenery in varying shades and textures to create a jungle look dotted with occasional bright spots of color.

2 Tropical plants grown in large decorative pots are conveniently portable for easy care while adding a lush look to expansive, shaded patios and outdoor living areas.

3 Plants with very large leaves are the most vulnerable to wind damage, which causes discoloration and shredded edges.

4 Strap leaf New Zealand flax and cordylines, popular for modern gardens, are not tolerant of our high summer heat and therefore should be used only as short-lived seasonal annuals or avoided altogether.

5 The gardens of Brasilian landscape architect Roberto Burle Marx are the best examples of designs well suited to our mid-century homes.

THE TREES

In the desert, palms and mesquite are the universal symbol of water. Even if water is not visible on the surface, trees prove it is abundant underground. It lies beneath dry washes, along the fault line, and at isolated springs that disappear beneath the sands over summer.

Early homesteads around the valley were thick with trees. Fluffy-headed tamarisk from the North African desert became the standard for shade and windbreak. These trees so willing to grow despite the extreme heat and drought have evolved in ways that make them pariahs in the modern landscape. Oddly enough, that feature which we seek will ultimately spell its demise.

This exotic tree, *Tamarix aphylla*, was introduced to the United States in the nineteenth century. Like many species from arid regions of the world, they are greedy water-finders with extensive roots that are key to its drought resistance. A single mature tamarisk can consume up to 300 gallons of ground water a day.

In the Coachella Valley Preserve, one colony of tamarisk trees matured as the roots fed on groundwater. It is believed their heavy demand caused a local spring to dry up, a water source vital to wildlife. The paradox is that while exotics like tamarisk can give life through shelter, they can take life by demanding water in the end.

In today's landscape, it's important to remember the tamarisk when choosing a species. Desert trees equipped for such arid conditions are by their very nature difficult on the small-scale cultivated landscape. But trees are so vital we cannot omit them for they create comfort outdoors and provide shade that enhances energy conservation in our homes. Therefore, with years required to achieve maturity, choosing the right tree is an important decision. There is rarely an opportunity to get it right the second time.

OPPOSITE: *Olea europea*

Albert Frey, the famous Palm Springs mid-century modern architect designed for passive solar benefits. A passive solar home keeps the south side open to the sun when it is low in the south sky in the winter. The sun warms spaces indoors, and slab floors that act as a thermal mass hold it into the evening. In summer the sun moves further north leaving these windows free of direct sun to keep interior spaces cooler. To maximize passive solar design in any home, beware of over-shading the south side in winter. A deciduous tree is more compatible with the concept, for it will be leafless in the winter to allow 80 to 90% of the sunlight through its bare branches.

TREES, SEASONS, EXPOSURE, AND CANOPY REDUCTION

Whether you are a year-round resident or a seasonal one influences how you view trees in the landscape. Seasonal homeowners crave the sunshine in those short winter days when they reside here. Their need for shade is minimal and the desire for a wholly-exposed homesite is understandable. If trees do pre-exist, the seasonal resident is likely to have the canopy thinned to make it as transparent as possible.

Trees are vital to year-round residents who spend the long, hot summer in the desert. Trees are the only way to create large-scale shaded outdoor spaces. A tree can render a space usable for outdoor living in the off season. Tree shade can reduce the amount of heat absorbed by buildings and paving beneath the canopy. Shade helps keep patio covers cooler, thereby reducing the amount of heat radiated into the spaces beneath. Swamp coolers in the shade maintain lower temperatures overall. Shaded air conditioners and ducting are more able to reduce temperatures indoors; energy consumption is significantly reduced as well. Plastics and woods maintain a much longer life if protected from UV exposure.

In order to maximize the shading potential of a tree, pay particular attention to the position of the sun around June 21, the summer solstice. This is its northernmost position in the sky. The shadow a tree casts at this time of year will be most vital to cooling in the hot months.

For winter residents, the gauge of shadow position should be about December 21, the winter solstice. This tells you where you can expect the shade to fall in order to be sure it doesn't affect outdoor living in the coolest time of year. You will need some influence from its canopy at the extremes of your stay: early fall and late spring.

Knowing your shading needs at the coldest and warmest time of year will dictate where the tree should be located for best results. It also helps you decide the optimal height and diameter of the tree canopy to achieve these goals in the space provided.

Wind is significant, particularly in Desert Hot Springs, North Palm Springs, and the communities located in the "wind belt" that runs down the center of the Coachella Valley. If older homes in this area have trees, they are often misshapen according to the prevailing wind.

This everyday wind stress is too much for most trees, even desert-adapted ones. The wind draws moisture out of the leaves so rapidly, the tree cannot replace it fast enough to keep the foliage green. This explains the near total absence of all but tamarisk and desert willow in some problem neighborhoods.

In the transitional seasons of spring and fall there is a higher incidence of extreme winds. These are more widespread and can originate in the west or east end of the valley. Home landscapes that otherwise experience little wind can be bruised and battered by these windstorms.

Because trees stand above the rooftops, they are more extensively impacted by wind than any other plant. They must be naturally strong-branching to avoid breakage in a gale.

Be aware that wind and trees also influence yard maintenance. Knowing the prevailing wind direction helps you site the tree. Trees upwind from swimming pools and intensely used outdoor living areas become a litter nightmare. Try instead to position trees downwind from the pool. Avoid jacaranda and Chilean mesquite altogether because their fine leaves disintegrate in the water, clogging filters.

Canopy reduction is the act of reducing the overall volume of a tree. It's a widespread practice to protect people, buildings, and vehicles from limbs broken from trees in windstorms. When done properly, canopy reduction preserves the natural branching form of the tree. This is a more expensive, laborious process because the pruner must always be assessing the structure of the tree as they cut to ensure an attractive result. The tree will tolerate this well and will slowly return to its former density.

Indiscriminate canopy reduction or "topping" is faster and cheaper. It requires no artistic assessment. Trimmers simply remove the top two thirds of the tree like a flat-top hair cut. While it may seem more cost effective, trees will respond to such butchery by producing adventitious growth. This produces rank, notoriously weak-jointed stems that are subject to a higher incidence of breakage. In the end the canopy returns more quickly and in ever-greater density. For the tree trimmer, topping ensures steady work removing excessive adventitious growth year after year.

Careful thinning of the young Chilean mesquite tree canopy helps to reduce wind resistance without spoiling its overall form.

⚠ AVOID PANCAKE ROOTS WITH SUMPS

Trees root only where they find water. When a tree is grown in a home lawn or golf course, it is watered by sprinklers that feed the turf grass. The grass sucks up most of the water so trees root right under the turf to gobble up all they can. They are less inclined to root deeply, which better anchors the tree. As a result the tree root system resembles a giant pancake with the trunk at the center. When subject to high winds, the pancake roots cannot hold tight enough to withstand the sheer pressure, particularly when the ground is soft after a drenching rain.

To help trees root deeply from the start, it's a wise practice to install simple do-it-yourself underground sumps. These help water move directly to the bottom of the root ball and beyond, where it remains unaffected by surface evaporation. This can be done in both turf lawns and standard bedding areas as well as parking lots and open space.

A sump is constructed of a 3-inch diameter perforated drainage pipe buried on end in a post hole 3 to 4 feet deep. The pipe can be filled with water at any time. Gravity drives it downward to flood the bottom of the root ball. Sumps may be piped into an automatic sprinkler system, so every time the system turns on the tree is deep watered within the sump.

With this deep water source in place, trees will root more securely, proving far more stable in the winds. This reduces the need to thin the canopy, allowing it to grow wider to shade a proportionately larger area.

TREES FOR OUR VALLEY

To the untrained eye, most trees appear identical. Too often they are lumped together alphabetically in the references and ganged at the garden center. To help you see the various roles individual species can play on your homesite or project, the best candidates have been divided into groups here. The groups help you know the best application, and make it easy to compare them on an even playing field.

Trees with bold flowers are rare in the desert and deserve high profile locations. These make exceptional single accents. Those with weeping character are some of the most romantic forms because they become more animated in a gentle desert breeze. Evergreen species are unique because they are in leaf all year-round to block the sun, and an unsightly neighbor, in every season. Finally the mesquites and palo verdes are in a class of their own due to their extreme desert adaptation.

TREES WITH BOLD FLOWERS

Bauhinia blakeana | **Hong Kong Orchid Tree** | 20' tall, 15' wide | Semi-deciduous | The Orchid Tree Inn in old Palm Springs was named for this beautiful species, many of which live on its grounds. No other tree compares with the large magenta pink flowers that adorn them in midwinter. The blooms are followed by pea-like pods filled with seeds that readily self-sow. These seedlings can exhibit genetic variability producing pink and lavender flowers far less vivid than the species. However, their sheer abundance and the resilience of these tropical trees combined with their beautiful round leaves nearly identical to those of the redbud, make them the highlight of the spring garden.

LEFT AND ABOVE: *Bauhinia blakeana*

Chilopsis linearis | **Desert Willow** | 25' tall and wide | Dotting the wash up to the Indian Canyons are large, bushy desert willows, the haunts of hummingbirds and rabbits sleeping out the heat of the day. These vivid green specimens contrast markedly with those out near windy point where they are battered by gale forces into scruffy gnarled forms. This native that survives the wind farm bears large tubular flowers that resemble purple foxglove. They bloom during the hot months from late spring through fall. In recent years Arid Zone Trees, an Arizona grower that distributes through Randy G. Myers & Nurseries in Sky Valley, has produced some truly excellent hybrids with larger flowers, bearing more intense colors. The variety 'AZT Bi-Color' produces burgundy petals accented with a magenta pink throat. Deep lavender, almost reddish-purple flowers distinguish 'AZT Desert Amethyst' and 'Burgundy' giving them a truly upscale character from the native. Use desert willow with single or multiple trunks as an accent tree in dry desert landscaping. Plant them near living areas to appreciate their exquisite flowers and the wildlife that attends them.

Jacaranda mimosifolia | **Jacaranda** | 30–50' tall, 24' wide | Semi-deciduous |

When the jacarandas bloom around the valley they are stand-out gorgeous. Vivid wisteria-purple blossoms cover the canopy at spring's end. While these are exceptional trees in bloom, the rest of the year they can be problematic. Fast growth and overall size make them poor choices for smaller homesites. Canopy reduction only stimulates more rank growth in this species. The fern-like leaves and hard silver-dollar sized seed pods create a perpetual litter problem. However, as accents for large estate properties, no other tree performs so well at a distance as a bold seasonal focal point.

ABOVE: *Schinus molle*

BELOW: *Acacia stenophylla* close up

TREES WITH WEEPING CHARACTER

Schinus molle | **California Pepper** | 35' tall, 20' wide | Evergreen | This is an historic tree associated with the mission era of California and therefore belongs with vintage Spanish style homes. It is slow-growing, aromatic, and intensely romantic. Beautiful light-green foliage makes this a superior choice for sheltered locations, allowing good control over horizontal light penetration. Occasional canopy reduction to prevent wind damage to brittle joints is all these beauties ask for. Not suited to full wind exposure.

Parkinsonia aculeata | **Mexican Palo Verde** | 30' tall and wide | Semi-deciduous | This desert native produces wispy thread-like foliage which offers minimal shade. Modern garden designers use its transparency and fine texture against colored walls for a feast of shadows and flashes of hue. As one of the most heavy-blooming palo verdes, it is virtually covered in beautiful golden spring flowers.

Acacia stenophylla | **Shoestring Wattle** | 40' tall, 20' wide | Evergreen | This wispy Australian acacia, valued for its more columnar form, makes it an excellent choice for smaller-sized homesites. Fine textured foliage, almost needles, dangle in a most graceful way. The tree retains an attractive pendulous character into old age unlike the former favorite, *Acacia saligna*, which tends to become woody and sparse with time. This tree is also preferred in the spare modern landscape for its semitransparency. Showy yellow flowers in spring.

EVERGREEN TREES

Olea europea | **Olive** | 35' tall, 30' wide |

The olive tree is one of Europe's greatest gifts to California. In the landscape few trees offer such character on so little water. Sadly, the old olive trees of Palm Springs are regularly sheared into hat boxes and lollipops to remove blooms and messy black fruit that follows. Not only does shearing spoil the beauty of the olive, it is a maintenance-intensive practice that must be repeated constantly to keep the trees in form. The new 'Swan Hill' and 'Majestic Beauty' fruitless olives solve this problem because they either lack flowers or pollen. These have now been in cultivation long enough to make large specimen-sized boxed trees available for new landscapes. For the Mediterranean-inspired home, there is nothing better to line a drive, shade a courtyard, or provide a view-sparing tree for the landscape. And under night lighting, there are few trees that compare.

Once an olive tree is sheared into a topiary-like hatbox or poodle, it can never regain its natural character. Poodled trees like the one above must be sheared often to keep them looking good while the natural multiple trunk form below may require a single annual canopy thinning to remove developing fruit. Fruitless olives require no trimming at all.

ABOVE: *Pinus halepensis*

BELOW: Ficus is the most versatile of all evergreens. Here it is shown with the trunks exposed in a hedge form illustrating how easily it can be shaped to serve a variety of needs from shade to screening.

Pinus halepensis | **Aleppo Pine** | 60' tall, 40' wide | Evergreen | This pine is native to northern Africa and is named for Aleppo, Syria, where it is widely grown. It is the only pine to grow well in the Coachella Valley. Capable of withstanding wind and drought, it survives problem areas of our wind belt. There the growth tends to be stubby and gnarled compared to the open-headed specimens you'll find in neighborhoods protected from wind by mountains. To know what to expect with Aleppo pine, take a look around your neighborhood to see what kind of shape they take. This will tell you if yours will attain the size and density you need.

Grevillea robusta | **Silk Oak** | 50' tall, 25' wide | Evergreen | This unique tree from Australia features a tall, nearly columnar form. It is used in condominium and apartment complexes for softening the ends of tall multistory buildings. However, if not provided adequate water they are known to die back at the top or a main branch will brown out. Generous watering encourages more deeper green foliage as well. The trees bloom in the higher branches with exotic bunches of golden flowers adapted to a curved-beak nectar feeding bird of its homeland.

Ficus microcarpa | **Indian Laurel Fig** | 30' tall, 25' wide | Evergreen | In the Palm Springs Movie Colony, some really old estates are enclosed by huge, old hedges of these trees. They bear big fat trunks that attest to the natural size of this species. Invariably when planted along streets, pools, and buildings, they are sheared like the olive into hat box shapes or topped within an inch of their lives. When used as hedges they are sheared often to maintain a more manageable size. These suffered the most frost damage in the 2006–07 freeze while those unsheared in any way, and bearing large natural canopies experienced only limited tip dieback. While this produces one of the most dense canopies for shading homes, the aggressive roots typical of most figs combined with the enormous size makes them a long-term problem for smaller lots.

Schinus terebinthifolius | **Brazilian Pepper** | 30' tall, 30' wide | Evergreen |
This cousin of the California pepper is a strong, upright tree that adapts exceptionally well to the desert. Under ordinary irrigation or beside lawns, the tree grows very quickly and can become a wind resistance problem. They are occasionally cut back to stumps, which spoils the natural branching. It is far more attractive periodically thinned to retain a natural canopy. They flower in the fall emitting a pungent scent, then produce red pepper-like berries on female trees.

THE PALO VERDES

These trees are natives of dry washes throughout the American Southwest, Mexico, and Central America. The Spanish name, *palo verde* translates to "green stick," describing the gorgeous green bark of trees in this genus. To maximize visibility of the trunks, growers prune for multi-trunk forms which not only widen the canopy, but add sculptural value under night lighting. All bloom bright yellow in the spring followed by pea-like seed pods which can present a significant litter problem. Pods and flowers offer high wildlife value. Regular pruning helps to expose more of the green trunk and lower branches.

ABOVE: *Cercidium floridum*

BELOW: *Cercidium praecox*

Cercidium floridum | **Blue Palo Verde** | 30' tall and wide | This largest tree of the species has stems and leaflets that are blue-green in color.

Cercidium microphyllum | **Foothills Palo Verde** | 20' tall and wide |
May serve as a large shrub or small tree. Better choice for city homes. Most drought-resistant species suited to rocky hillsides.

Cercidium praecox | **Sonoran Palo Verde** | 25' tall and wide | Produces the brightest green bark of all. Long semi-weeping foliage is sculptural. Excellent medium size suited to a wide range of homesites.

Prosopis chilensis

THE MESQUITES

The wickedly thorny screwbean mesquite (*Prosopis pubescens*) can be found in the canyons all around the Coachella Valley. It's a shrubby tree that grows up to about 15 feet, which isn't well suited to the average yard. However, it remains a vital component in large-scale wildlife-oriented landscapes.

The mesquites listed below are well established in southwestern landscapes and make outstanding shade trees. They bloom yellow in spring, followed by highly-nutritious pods and seeds, once a vital food source to Native Americans. Mesquites become semi-deciduous in the low desert.

Prosopis chilensis | **Chilean Mesquite** | 25' tall and wide | Perhaps the most beautiful of all mesquites, this tree is found in parking lots everywhere. Wide branching but weak due to fast growth, the canopies are annually thinned to encourage greater structural integrity.

Prosopis alba | **Argentine Mesquite** | 25' tall and wide | More cold-hardy choice for the east valley and high desert.

Prosopis glandulosa | **Honey Mesquite, Texas Mesquite** | 25' tall, 30' wide | This tree is the largest and most cold-hardy choice, native to the dry prairie states and ideal for the high desert. Produces large 5-inch-long leathery pods with a notably sweet flavor.

LOCATION:

RANDY G. MYERS & NURSERIES AND TREE SALVAGE

For the past thirty years, Randy Myers has been a mover and shaker in Coachella Valley horticulture. He is a primary desert tree authority. His work is little known to the public but famous among professionals because the operation had strictly been wholesale until recently.

The 20-acre growing ground is located off Dillon Road in Sky Valley and contains thousands of specimen trees, cacti, and other desert plants. Many of them were salvaged from sites all around the valley. Some are stored in ground at the yard, others boxed, and smaller ones potted and preserved for future sale. Other trees and plants are grown from parent stock well-proven in our climate, so the offspring are raised to be locally adapted from the start. Randy and his crews were instrumental in relocating all the large palo verde trees to the Bighorn Canyons, and his plants are scattered across the valley in hundreds of high-profile landscapes. While still largely a wholesale operation, Randy G. Myers & Nurseries is open by appointment to select retail customers wishing to add large specimen trees or cacti to their landscape. You can hand-select the plant perfect for your needs at the yard, then the nursery crew will transport and transplant it at your site.

Randy G. Myers & Nurseries and Tree Salvage
21100 Hot Springs Road
Sky Valley, CA 92241
(760) 329-8757

THIS CHAPTER
IN A NUTSHELL

1. A single tamarisk tree can consume up to 300 gallons of groundwater in a single day.

2. Position trees with respect to the sun's position at midwinter and midsummer to determine where shadows will be cast within your homesite.

3. Deep-water roots with sumps and bubblers to prevent surface rooting and promote increased drought resistance.

4. Before choosing a tree in very windy parts of the valley, study the neighborhood to learn what species will survive there and to what height you can expect them to grow under local conditions.

5. In reducing an overly large or dense tree, it is far better to thin and shape the canopy rather than implement radical "topping" which spoils its natural beauty and stimulates more rapid regrowth.

CHAPTER 10

STYLE GUIDE PLANT LISTS

A surprising range of architectural styles exist throughout the Coachella Valley. Each one is unique in its own way and projects a distinct character. When designers create the landscape for a house, they take into consideration the architectural style in order to create outdoor spaces that complement it. An important step in the design process is to create a list of plants that become the signatures of the style. The entire landscape is not restricted to these plants, though. Their presence is there to establish a more concise connection between the outdoor spaces, the building, and interior spaces.

This collection of plants is known as a "palette." Just as a painter creates a palette of colors to create a scene, the plant palette provides the coordinated species of the landscape designer.

MO'S TOP TEN PLANT PICKS

SPANISH

This is the original architectural style in the desert, composed of the earth itself and very little timber. Plants are rugged and resilient, and come out of the Mexican gardens from which most of early, arid California evolved.

1	*Agave angustifolia*	**Agave**	Succulent	page 97
2	*Opuntia ficus indica*	**Prickly Pear**	Succulent	page 47
3	*Bougainvillea* **hybrid**	**Bougainvillea**	Shrub/vine	pages 59–61
4	*Cuphea llavea*	**Bat Faced Cuphea**	Perennial	page 83
5	*Antigonon leptopus*	**Queen's Wreath**	Vine	page 88
6	*Lantana* **hybrids**	**Bush Lantana**	Shrub	pages 67–68
7	*Jacaranda mimosifolia*	**Jacaranda**	Tree	page 125
8	*Schinus molle*	**California Pepper**	Tree	page 126
9	*Caesalpinia pulcherrima*	**Mexican Bird of Paradise**	Tree	page 66
10	*Salvia greggii*	**Autumn Sage**	Perennial	page 62

Materials Palette: Saltillo pavers, bright Mexican tiles, colored gravels, tier fountain, large carved cantera stone figures, faux pre-Columbian statuary, Moroccan lanterns, chiminea, thatched palapa, rustic wood furniture, wrought iron, Ecipale chairs.

MID-CENTURY MODERN

This style established by world renowned architects Donald Wexler and Albert Frey emphasizes very simple buildings open to the outdoors. With space-age block, steel and glass, this is a sculptural landscape that depends on bold architectural plants to create living art in the garden.

1	*Beaucarnea recurvata*	**Ponytail Palm**	Tree/shrub	page 109
2	*Carissa grandiflora*	**Natal Plum**	Shrub	page 112
3	*Portulacaria afra*	**Jade Tree**	Succulent	page 35
4	*Sanseveria trifasciata*	**Mother In Law Tongue**	Succulent	page 110
5	*Agave victoriae-reginae*	**Queen Victoria Agave**	Succulent	page 99
6	*Kalanchoe thyrsiflora*	**Flapjacks**	Shrub	page 35
7	*Echinocactus grusonii*	**Golden Barrel Cactus**	Succulent	page 53
8	*Gazania* clumping hybrids	**Gazania**	Biennial	page 84
9	*Alluadia procera*	**Alluadia**	Succulent	page 36
10	*Acacia stenophylla*	**Shoestring Wattle**	Tree	page 126

Materials Palette: Concrete and block, glass tile, small mosaic tile fields and water features, light bottom pool, clean-colored surfaces, fields of colored gravel, curvilinear edging treatments, translucent panels, metallic accents, colored glass architectural lighting, graphic sconce lighting, shade sails, metal street numbers, sleek and minimalist style furniture.

BIGHORN NATURAL

Made of stone and sand, nestled into the desert itself, this style derived from the look of ancient cliff-dwellings is perhaps the most naturalistic of all building styles. With the emphasis on wildlife and wildland, this palette is strongly native, rugged, and reflects the very nature of the desert itself.

1	*Nassella tenuissima*	**Mexican Feather Grass**	Grass	page 71
2	*Washingtonia filifera*	**California Fan Palm**	Tree	page 19
3	*Aloe vera*	**Medicine Aloe**	Succulent	page 31
4	*Ferocactus cylindraceus*	**Compass Barrel**	Cactus	page 44
5	*Echinocereus engelmannii*	**Hedgehog Cactus**	Cactus	page 44
6	*Opuntia basilaris*	**Beavertail Prickly Pear Cactus**	Cactus	page 45
7	*Encelia farinosa*	**Brittlebush**	Perennial	page 85
8	*Hesperaloe parviflora*	**Red Yucca**	Succulent	page 100
9	*Agave deserti*	**Desert Agave**	Succulent	page 98
10	*Fouquieria splendens*	**Ocotillo**	Shrub	page 101

Materials Palette: Sandstone paving, natural rock walls, curbs and retaining walls, dark pebble bottom pool, high-volume boulder waterfalls, monolithic carved stone water features in pebble field, wildlife sculpture (figurative and abstract), rustic round stock shade structure.

DESERT MODERN

This uniquely contemporary look is a hybrid between naturalistic hues and the rigid simplistic forms of the modern movement. Buildings dominate and planting is less emphasized than with other styles. Therefore the palette is a blending of the Bighorn natural and mid-century modern with hints of international influences

1	*Cycas revoluta*	Sago Palm	Shrub	page 22
2	*Aloe dichotoma*	Kokerboom	Succulent	page 30
3	*Kalanchoe beharensis*		Succulent	page 34
4	*Pachypodium lamerei*	Pachypodium	Succulent	page 36
5	*Pennisetum setaceum*	Fountain Grass	Perennial	page 70
6	*Yucca rostrata*	Beaked Yucca	Succulent	page 94
7	*Dasilirion longissimum*	Mexican Grass Tree	Succulent	page 100
8	*Cassia artemisioides*	Feathery Cassia	Shrub	page 104
9	*Agave geminiflora*	Agave	Succulent	page 98
10	*Prosopis chilensis*	Chilean Mesquite	Tree	page 130

Materials Palette: Stucco, concrete block, poured paving, modern metals, dark bottom pool, minimalist water features, oversized boulders, graphic shade sails, gravel fields, architectural plant specimens, sleek European furniture.

MEDITERRANEAN

Soft and subtle defines this architecture derived from the arid regions of the Old World mired in the ruins of classical civilizations. Planting for this landscape is quietly colorful, highly aromatic, and evokes the look and feel of southern Europe and Asia minor.

1	*Phoenix dactylifera*	**Date Palm**	Tree	page 21
2	*Olea europea*	**Fruitless Olive**	Tree	page 127
3	*Salvia leucantha*	**Mexican Bush Sage**	Perennial	page 86
4	*Spaheralcea ambigua*	**Globe Mallow**	Perennial	page 87
5	*Leonotis leonurus*	**Lion's Tail**	Shrub	page 88
6	*Agave desmettiana*	**Agave**	Succulent	page 98
7	*Leucophyllum frutescens*	**Texas Ranger**	Shrub	page 69
8	*Rosmarinus officinalis*	**Rosemary**	Shrub	
9	*Chilopsis linearis*	**Desert Willow**	Tree	page 124
10	*Yucca recurvifolia*	**Recurved Yucca**	Succulent	page 94

Materials Palette: Terra cotta, topiary, hewn granite-like stone paving, decomposed granite ground plain, plaster, tier fountain, tile, wrought iron and glass furniture, colorful tile mosaic table tops.

TROPICAL

Few styles thwart the heat and glare of the desert like the lush tropical appeal of equatorial jungles. Rich green foliage contrasting with vivid, hot-colored flowers combine elements of the South Pacific with the Mexican Riviera to create the true oasis that early Palm Springs residents sought to embody within the great walled estates.

1	*Arecastrum romanzoffianum*	Queen Palm	Tree	page 19
2	*Chamerops humilis*	Mediterranean Fan Palm	Shrub	page 20
3	*Tecoma stans* hybrids	Yellow Bells	Shrub	page 63
4	*Tecomaria capense*	Cape Honeysuckle	Shrub/vine	page 64
5	*Lantana camara*	Lantana	Shrub	page 68
6	*Bauhinia blakeana*	Hong Kong Orchid Tree	Tree	page 122
7	*Passiflora alato-caerulea*	Passion Flower Vine	Vine	page 113
8	*Hippeastrum vittatum*	Amaryllis	Perennial	page 114
9	*Macfadyena unguis-cati*	Cats Claw Creeper	Vine	page 113
10	*Strelitzia reginae*	Bird of Paradise	Perennial	page 109

Materials Palette: Thatch, natural flagstone, Tiki art, Asian art, Mexican art, bamboo or woven grass panels and fencing, gas or oil torch, fire pit, teak furniture with tropical prints.

SUNBELT'S SOUTHERN CALIFORNIA BOOKSHELF

Anza-Borrego: A Photographic Journey	Ernie Cowan
Anza-Borrego A to Z: People, Places, and Things	Diana Lindsay
Anza-Borrego Desert Region (Wilderness Press)	L. and D. Lindsay
California Desert Miracle: The Fight for Parks and Wilderness	Frank Wheat
Cycling Los Angeles	D. and S. Brundige
Cycling Orange County	D. and S. Brundige
Cycling the Palm Springs Region	Nelson Copp
Cycling San Diego	Copp, Schad
Desert Lore of Southern California	Choral Pepper
Fire, Chaparral, and Survival in Southern California	Richard W. Halsey
Fossil Treasures of the Anza-Borrego Desert	Jefferson, Lindsay
Geology of Anza-Borrego: Edge of Creation	Remeika, Lindsay
Guacamole Dip	Daniel Reveles
Marshal South and the Ghost Mountain Chronicles	Diana Lindsay
Mexican Slang Plus Graffiti	Linton Robinson
Mining History and Geology of Joshua Tree (SDAG)	Margaret Eggers, ed.
Palm Springs Legends: Creation of a Desert Oasis	Greg Niemann
Palm Springs Oasis: A Photographic Essay	Greg Lawson
Palm Springs-Style Gardening	Maureen Gilmer
Peaks, Palms, and Picnics: Day Journeys in The Coachella Valley	Linda Pyle
Spanish Lingo for the Savvy Gringo	Elizabeth Reid
Strangers in a Stolen Land: History of Indians in San Diego County	Richard Carrico
Tequila, Lemon and Salt	Daniel Reveles
This Day in California History	Carl Palm

Incorporated in 1988, with roots in publishing since 1973, Sunbelt Publications produces and distributes natural science and outdoor guidebooks, regional histories and pictorials, and stories that celebrate the land and its people.

Sunbelt books help to discover and conserve the natural, historical, and cultural heritage of unique regions on the frontiers of adventure and learning. Our books guide readers into distinctive communities and special places, both natural and man-made.

We carry hundreds of books on southern California!

Visit us online at:

www.sunbeltbooks.com